Puzzles Plus Somet

THIS BOOK IS PACKED WITH OVER 80 WORD SEARCH PUZZLES. UNLIKE TYPICAL WORD SEARCHES, EACH OF THESE PUZZLES FOCUSES ON A CLASSIC FBI CASE. YOU'LL LEARN SOMETHING ABOUT THE CASE AS YOU SOLVE THE PUZZLE. THE PUZZLES ARE STILL IN A FAMILIAR FORMAT. LETTERS ARE PLACED IN A GRID, AND THE WORDS IN THE LIST CAN BE FOUND IN A STRAIGHT LINE VERTICALLY, HORIZONTALLY, OR DIAGONALLY. WORDS MAY READ EITHER FORWARD OR BACKWARD.

ONE OF THE MOST POPULAR WAYS TO TACKLE A WORD SEARCH IS TO ISOLATE A LETTER, SCAN THE LINES TO FIND AN INSTANCE OF THE LETTER, THEN SCAN THE ADJOINING LETTERS TO SEE IF THE WORD CAN BE FORMED. THERE ARE A COUPLE DIFFERENT WAYS TO DO THIS, AND PUZZLE ENTHUSIASTS ARE DIVIDED ON WHETHER IT'S MORE HELPFUL TO FOCUS ON THE FIRST LETTER OF THE WORD OR ON AN UNCOMMON LETTER. EXPERIMENTATION CAN HELP YOU GRASP THE STRATEGY THAT BEST SUITS YOU. LIKEWISE, SEARCHING FOR DOUBLE LETTERS CAN ASSIST IN PINPOINTING A LOCATION. SO HAVE FUN, LEARN SOMETHING NEW, AND GIVE YOUR BRAIN A LIGHT WORKOUT!

ANSWERS CAN BE FOUND IN THE BACK OF THE BOOK.

Notorious

ABETTED
ADVANTAGE
ARM
ASSASSINATION
ATTAIN
CLEANING
CONTROL
DEMISE
EMPLOYEE
GANG
GARAGE
IMMIGRANT
INFLUENTIAL
INTERESTS
LABOR
LIEUTENANT
MASSACRE
MOB
NOTORIOUS
NULLIFIED
PERIOD
PROHIBITION
PUBLIC
QUIT
RACKET
REPUTATION
RIVAL
SCHOOL
STREET
SUBURB
SURRENDER
VIOLENT

Born in Brooklyn, New York, in 1899, Al Capone became one of the most notorious criminals in U.S. history, developing a reputation as a ruthless mob boss. His violent tactics are perhaps best reflected in the infamous 1929 St. Valentine's Day Massacre, when Capone's associates gunned down a rival gang in a Chicago garage.

BRAIN GAMES®

FBI

WORD SEARCH PUZZLES

Publications International, Ltd.

Images from Shutterstock.com

Louis Weber, CEO
Publications International, Ltd.
8140 Lehigh Avenue
Morton Grove, IL 60053

ISBN: 978-1-64558-637-1

Manufactured in China.

8 7 6 5 4 3 2 1

D	F	D	T	I	U	Q	N	U	L	L	I	F	I	E	D	D
C	M	P	E	C	H	E	M	P	L	O	Y	E	E	L	S	E
N	I	Q	M	M	E	G	A	T	N	A	V	D	A	I	U	T
O	M	L	N	O	I	T	I	B	I	H	O	R	P	N	O	T
I	M	T	B	L	B	S	S	C	H	O	O	L	L	T	I	E
T	I	O	E	U	A	O	E	M	Y	N	Z	I	Y	E	R	B
A	G	D	T	K	P	I	R	T	W	U	E	E	L	R	O	A
N	R	M	G	H	C	A	T	S	N	U	J	H	A	E	T	C
I	A	T	A	X	R	A	Z	N	T	E	Q	C	V	S	O	L
S	N	H	N	S	S	T	R	E	E	T	L	S	I	T	N	E
S	T	I	G	N	S	T	N	R	U	U	I	O	R	S	I	A
A	R	E	P	U	T	A	T	I	O	N	L	O	I	G	B	N
S	Z	R	I	M	N	I	C	T	G	B	T	F	A	V	E	I
S	F	L	B	T	G	N	L	R	W	J	A	R	N	A	O	N
A	L	H	I	Y	V	M	F	Q	E	L	A	L	J	I	N	G
Q	R	E	D	N	E	R	R	U	S	G	D	O	I	R	E	P
A	L	O	R	T	N	O	C	R	E	B	S	U	B	U	R	B

Soon after, the FBI began investigating his actions, and he was ultimately charged and found guilty of tax evasion. He spent seven years in prison, but deteriorating health prevented him from returning to the mob after his release. Capone died in Florida in 1947.

Answers on page 172.

The Case of Ana Montes

AGENTS	DETECTION	NOTHING
ANALYST	EVERYTHING	POLICIES
BUILD	EXPERT	RADIO
CAUSE	FOREIGN	RECRUITMENT
CLASSIFIED	HANDLER	SECRETS
COLLEAGUE	HAPPEN	SUSPICION
COMMUNITY	IDENTIFY	TERRORIST
COPY	IDEOLOGY	UNCOVER
COUNTRY	JOB	VIEWS
COVERT	LAPTOP	YEARS
DAYS	LEAKING	

Ana Montes began her career in 1984 with the Department of Justice in Washington D.C., where she often spoke of her disagreements with U.S. foreign policy, especially concerning Central America. Her outspoken opinions caught the attention of Cuban officials, who recruited her as a spy.

S	W	E	I	V	S	E	I	C	I	L	O	P	V	R	Y	J
K	G	N	I	H	T	Y	R	E	V	E	E	X	P	E	R	T
J	A	R	R	R	N	C	O	M	M	U	N	I	T	Y	T	J
Q	H	T	N	Y	G	O	L	O	E	D	I	A	D	N	N	F
L	Z	G	N	I	H	T	O	N	D	A	Y	S	E	E	U	C
A	D	E	I	F	I	S	S	A	L	C	W	M	T	K	O	R
P	L	P	V	Q	H	H	R	R	C	J	T	X	E	D	C	F
T	F	H	E	Q	G	A	N	O	E	I	G	P	C	L	N	O
O	Z	X	E	S	D	Y	L	O	U	V	T	C	T	I	E	R
P	S	G	H	I	U	L	F	R	I	S	O	Y	I	U	P	E
A	X	R	O	A	E	A	C	I	Y	C	A	C	O	B	P	I
Y	G	L	A	A	N	E	C	L	T	N	I	O	N	C	A	G
N	T	E	G	E	R	D	A	N	Z	N	G	P	D	U	H	N
G	S	U	N	J	Y	N	L	P	B	B	E	Y	S	W	H	F
E	E	G	O	T	A	T	R	E	V	O	C	D	S	U	X	Z
V	D	B	O	T	S	I	R	O	R	R	E	T	I	B	S	Z
S	T	E	R	C	E	S	L	E	A	K	I	N	G	G	K	G

She got a job at the Defense Intelligence Agency, which afforded her the opportunity to pass along classified information to the Cuban government for more than a decade. In 2000, after a coworker became suspicious, the FBI opened an investigation on Montes, and discovered evidence of her actions. She was arrested 10 days after the 9/11 attacks, and sentenced to 25 years in prison.

Answers on page 172.

The Martin Durkin Manhunt

ALARM
ATROCIOUS
BANDIT
CHICAGO
CONFIDENTIAL
COURT
DAYLIGHT
DESERT
EFFECT
EXPIRATION
FEDERAL
FIELDS
FUGITIVE
GARAGE
INACCURATE
LUGGAGE
OVERCOAT
PENITENTIARY
PHOTOGRAPH
POLICE
PURPOSE
RACKET
RAILROAD
REVOLVER
REWARD
RUSE
STOLEN
SYSTEM
TERM
TOURING
VIOLATION
WOUNDED

On October 11, 1925, FBI Special Agent Edwin C. Shanahan became the first FBI agent killed in the line of duty. Shanahan had attempted to apprehend Martin Durkin, a known automobile thief who was also wanted for shooting four police officers. But when Shanahan confronted Durkin at a Chicago garage, the thief pulled a gun and shot the agent in the chest.

Y	T	P	X	Y	R	A	I	T	N	E	T	I	N	E	P	T
F	I	C	D	R	U	S	E	V	I	T	I	G	U	F	I	M
W	I	N	E	T	N	Y	B	T	R	E	S	E	D	D	Y	T
T	R	E	A	F	D	A	Y	L	I	G	H	T	N	E	N	A
M	E	A	L	C	F	T	O	N	H	O	D	A	R	C	O	O
L	P	R	I	D	C	E	O	P	E	B	B	C	K	O	I	C
U	S	O	M	L	S	U	A	U	R	L	O	X	G	U	T	R
G	W	N	L	Q	R	R	R	E	R	N	O	A	X	R	A	E
G	O	O	N	I	G	O	V	A	F	I	C	T	K	T	L	V
A	E	L	U	O	C	L	A	I	T	I	N	P	S	V	O	O
G	V	G	T	N	O	E	D	D	H	E	M	G	E	M	I	S
E	W	O	A	V	D	E	G	C	S	Y	S	T	E	M	V	V
F	H	V	E	R	N	E	E	X	P	I	R	A	T	I	O	N
P	E	R	A	T	A	H	D	P	T	E	S	O	P	R	U	P
G	E	H	I	B	M	G	T	C	A	P	T	E	K	C	A	R
D	R	A	W	E	R	O	Y	M	F	E	D	E	R	A	L	R
Z	L	A	L	A	R	M	U	S	U	O	I	C	O	R	T	A

Shanahan's murder sparked an FBI manhunt that spanned the country, as agents tracked Durkin's movements to Los Angeles, El Paso, and finally, St. Louis, where he was arrested as he attempted to flee by train. Durkin received a 35-year prison term, and was released in 1954.

Answers on page 172.

The Amerithrax Investigation

ANTHRAX	HISTORY	POSTAL
ATTACKS	IMPACT	POTENTIAL
BIOLOGICAL	INSPECTION	PROSECUTOR
BREAKTHROUGH	INVESTIGATORS	RECOVERY
COMPLEX	ISSUANCE	RESEARCH
CONTINENTS	JUSTICE	SECTION
DOCUMENTS	LABORATORY	TASK
ENFORCEMENT	LETTER	TECHNICIAN
ENSUING	LOCATION	TERRORIST
FORCE	MEDICAL	WORK
FUTURE	PARTNERS	

In the unsettling days that followed the 9/11 terrorist attacks, a new panic gripped the nation as envelopes laced with deadly anthrax started showing up in mailboxes. The FBI immediately began investigating the biological attack, which killed five people and sickened 17 others.

N	O	I	T	A	C	O	L	C	C	O	M	P	L	E	X	Y
F	B	E	I	J	D	O	C	U	M	E	N	T	S	T	V	R
S	T	N	E	N	I	T	N	O	C	A	T	T	A	C	K	S
F	B	S	C	R	K	A	N	T	H	R	A	X	T	A	S	K
N	R	U	R	E	F	R	O	T	U	C	E	S	O	R	P	T
A	E	I	O	T	U	L	A	I	T	N	E	T	O	P	R	T
I	A	N	F	T	T	T	E	R	R	O	R	I	S	T	J	T
C	K	G	D	E	U	S	D	H	C	R	A	E	S	E	R	N
I	T	H	I	L	R	I	N	S	P	E	C	T	I	O	N	E
N	H	I	N	V	E	S	T	I	G	A	T	O	R	S	L	M
H	R	S	Y	F	P	A	R	T	N	E	R	S	S	H	A	E
C	O	T	N	M	Y	R	E	V	O	C	E	R	E	X	T	C
E	U	O	L	A	B	O	R	A	T	O	R	Y	C	M	S	R
T	G	R	F	L	A	C	I	D	E	M	U	R	T	A	O	O
U	H	Y	I	S	S	U	A	N	C	E	U	K	I	P	P	F
I	M	P	A	C	T	L	A	C	I	G	O	L	O	I	B	N
O	J	J	U	S	T	I	C	E	K	R	O	W	N	E	A	E

Code-named Amerithrax, the investigation encompassed collecting thousands of environmental samples and interviewing witnesses on six continents. The search eventually led the FBI to the culprit, Dr. Bruce Ivins. While Ivins took his own life before charges could be filed, the FBI hunt resulted in new scientific breakthroughs that could continue to benefit future cases.

Answers on page 172.

The Teflon Don

ACQUITTALS	HENCHMAN	PRESSURE
AIRTIGHT	INTIMIDATION	RACKETEERING
BOSS	JURORS	REFUSED
CHARGE	LAW	SCENE
COUNTS	MAJOR	SLIPPERY
DAPPER	MOBSTER	SPILLED
DETECTIVE	NARCOTICS	SYNDICATES
DILIGENT	NICKNAME	TRADE
DUBBED	ORDERS	TRAFFICKING
EXPENSIVE	PLOT	UNDERCOVER
FAMILY	POWERFUL	

The first time the FBI arrested famous mobster John Gotti was in 1968. He was released after only a few years, then arrested again soon after. But Gotti always seemed able to evade serious prison time, even for grievous crimes, earning him the nickname "the Teflon Don." After yet another offense—the murder of his Gambino family rival Paul Castellano—the FBI and NYPD redoubled their efforts.

Z	X	Y	W	A	L	E	X	P	E	N	S	I	V	E	N	A
R	F	R	H	E	N	C	H	M	A	N	D	U	B	B	E	D
P	I	E	M	E	M	A	N	K	C	I	N	T	S	S	O	B
G	D	P	A	M	Q	T	R	A	F	F	I	C	K	I	N	G
N	N	P	J	U	N	O	I	T	A	D	I	M	I	T	N	I
Y	F	I	O	N	A	R	S	R	O	R	U	J	S	O	V	N
S	L	L	R	D	E	C	E	X	C	E	G	R	A	H	C	O
H	C	S	S	E	D	R	Q	T	D	E	S	U	F	E	R	E
U	Z	I	E	R	E	I	U	U	S	D	A	P	P	E	R	S
A	G	M	T	C	E	T	L	S	I	B	T	F	Q	R	P	R
I	C	S	A	O	T	N	E	I	S	T	O	O	M	X	O	E
R	O	P	C	V	C	R	E	K	G	E	T	M	L	V	W	D
T	U	I	I	E	L	R	A	C	C	E	R	A	F	P	E	R
I	N	L	D	R	G	P	A	D	S	A	N	P	L	A	R	O
G	T	L	N	B	X	N	V	N	E	E	R	T	S	S	F	L
H	S	E	Y	R	D	J	Y	L	I	M	A	F	B	P	U	Z
T	S	D	S	E	V	I	T	C	E	T	E	D	D	P	L	Q

Using electronic surveillance, undercover agents, and mob informants, the agencies were able to build a strong case against the mob boss. Finally, on April 2, 1992, Gotti was found guilty on 13 counts, including murder and racketeering. He died in prison in 2002.

 Answers on page 173.

The Demise of Enron

ACCOUNTABLE	COMPENSATE	INTERNAL
ACTIONS	CREATION	INTERVIEWS
BANKRUPTCY	DATA	INVESTORS
BLEND	ENERGY	MAGNITUDE
BOOST	EVIDENCE	MILLIONS
BOXES	EXCHANGE	MODEL
BUSINESS	FORCE	STREET
CHIEF	FOUR	TASK
COLLAPSE	FRAUD	TERABYTES
COMMUNITY	GIMMICKS	UNIQUE
COMPANY	HOUSTON	

When Houston-based energy-trading and utilities company Enron filed for bankruptcy in December 2001, investors and employees lost millions. The company's collapse led to the creation of the Enron Task Force, made up of investigators from the FBI, IRS, SEC, and the Department of Justice. They discovered that Enron officials, including the CEO, had been falsifying accounting numbers to make the company appear more appealing to investors.

L	E	A	T	S	O	O	B	R	C	O	M	P	A	N	Y	Y
E	S	E	D	U	T	I	N	G	A	M	S	E	H	F	H	C
D	P	R	S	T	R	E	E	T	C	N	A	T	C	Q	O	T
O	A	E	U	Q	I	N	U	U	C	L	B	A	S	J	U	P
M	L	Z	O	O	D	C	E	B	O	A	D	S	T	M	S	U
E	L	J	W	A	F	G	O	O	U	N	Q	N	Z	I	T	R
C	O	R	T	Y	N	X	T	I	N	R	C	E	E	L	O	K
R	C	A	S	A	E	S	N	S	T	E	H	P	E	L	N	N
O	X	L	H	S	N	V	E	Q	A	T	I	M	V	I	B	A
F	E	C	M	O	E	T	U	V	B	N	E	O	I	O	T	B
J	X	C	I	S	Y	Q	J	R	L	I	F	C	D	N	C	H
E	N	T	T	B	U	S	I	N	E	S	S	T	E	S	G	K
V	C	O	A	G	I	M	M	I	C	K	S	A	N	K	B	K
A	R	R	K	S	X	S	D	U	A	R	F	S	C	S	C	F
S	E	S	W	E	I	V	R	E	T	N	I	K	E	Y	O	E
T	E	E	N	E	R	G	Y	W	N	O	I	T	A	E	R	C
Y	T	I	N	U	M	M	O	C	I	Z	J	E	E	H	T	S

The task force sifted through 3,000 boxes of evidence and conducted 1,800 interviews during their investigation, which resulted in the convictions of almost the entire executive management team.

Answers on page 173.

1996 Summer Olympics Bomber

ADAMANT
BACKPACK
BARRELS
BINS
BOMBS
CADRE
CAVES
CREDIBLE
DEFEAT
DUMPSTER
DYNAMITE
ELUDE
FAMILIARITY
FOCUS
FOREST
GATHER
GROCERY
INJURIES
LAND
MANPOWER
OFFICER
OUTDOORSMAN
PERIOD
RUMMAGING
RURAL
SCOUTS
SURVIVALIST
SUSPECTED
TRASH
VEGETABLES
VULNERABLE
WINTER

The 1996 Summer Olympics are often remembered for a sobering reason. On July 27, a bomb was detonated in Centennial Olympic Park, killing one and injuring more than 100. Over the next two years, three more bombings occurred in Georgia and Alabama, with evidence pointing to outdoorsman Eric Rudolph as the culprit.

P	H	E	B	J	D	O	I	R	E	P	F	O	R	E	S	T
O	V	U	L	N	E	R	A	B	L	E	B	O	M	B	S	E
K	U	L	S	U	R	V	I	V	A	L	I	S	T	U	L	Y
L	I	T	D	H	V	N	O	L	A	R	U	R	Z	B	K	S
D	Z	N	D	H	S	S	E	S	U	C	O	F	I	H	N	E
Y	Z	K	J	O	O	F	F	I	C	E	R	D	L	Y	F	L
Y	T	I	C	U	O	D	D	E	T	C	E	P	S	U	S	B
R	R	I	A	A	R	R	S	L	E	R	R	A	B	W	M	A
E	E	U	R	T	P	I	S	Q	C	S	C	O	U	T	S	T
C	G	T	M	A	R	K	E	M	D	Y	N	A	M	I	T	E
O	C	N	N	M	I	E	C	S	A	S	G	Y	J	D	C	G
R	U	A	Z	I	A	L	W	A	T	N	H	A	S	O	A	E
G	E	M	V	O	W	G	I	O	B	A	E	S	T	P	D	V
N	L	A	M	E	D	E	I	M	P	O	E	L	A	H	R	P
C	E	D	N	N	S	O	M	N	A	N	F	F	U	R	E	K
G	M	A	A	V	S	D	H	R	G	F	A	D	E	D	T	R
H	B	L	R	E	T	S	P	M	U	D	R	M	W	D	E	R

But it would take five more years for authorities to close in on the skilled survivalist, who hid in the mountains of North Carolina. The FBI relentlessly pursued Rudolph, who was finally apprehended as he rummaged for food in a grocery store trash bin. He was sentenced to multiple life sentences without the possibility of parole.

Answers on page 173.

Marian Zacharski

AEROSPACE	ENGINEERING	OPERATIONS
ALIMONY	EUROPEAN	RACK
BETRAYAL	EVIDENCE	RADAR
CHARMING	EXPENSES	SCHEMATICS
CLEARANCE	IDEAL	SYSTEM
CLEVER	INDUSTRIAL	TURNCOAT
COINS	IRON	UNDERCOVER
COMPROMISED	MICROPHONE	VITAL
COOPERATE	MIRRORS	WORK
COUNTER	MISERY	
DEBT	MONEY	

When engineer William Holden Bell met sales rep Marian Zacharski, the two men struck up a fast friendship. Bell, who was divorced and struggling financially, especially appreciated his friend's offer to pay him for his technical expertise. But as time went on, Zacharski began demanding classified information about projects that Bell had worked on.

I L J O E X P E N S E S B Q T K C
M A C H A L I M O N Y U T B V E E
O I O H V E S A C W X R E A C N B
N R O R I X U C C H E D C N G A E
E T P E T K H R I V A O A I M G T
Y S E V A D S O O T M R N B E R R
I U R E L M W C P P A E M F D T A
D D A L O M R F R E E M C I U R Y
E N T C E E I O L R R A E R N A A
A I E S D C M C I M Q A N H E G L
L R C N R I N N R U E C T R C K I
E A U O S O G E K O O T O I R S I
W D S E U C R C D A P S S O O R F
L A D N B N A R T I P H W Y O N V
P R R L I R T Q I A V X O N S W S
D Z C Z C O D E C M M E O N D M M
M I S E R Y C E R P S E M G E R Y

Bell, desperate for money, obliged; but the FBI had been watching the pair for some time. They confronted Bell and convinced him to wear a wire to a meeting with his "friend," who turned out to be a Soviet spy. Zacharski was later arrested and sentenced to life in prison.

Answers on page 173.

Operation Shrouded Horizon

ADDITION
CHARGES
COMBAT
CYBER
DATA
DISMANTLE
DOMAIN
DOZENS
FACILITATED
FEARFUL
FORUM
HAVEN
INDICTMENTS
JURISDICTIONS
MAKE
MALWARE
OPERATORS
PASSWORD
PERPETRATORS
PRIME
PROLIFIC
RESOURCE
SEIZURE
SERVERS
SOFTWARE
STOLEN
TOOLS
TRANSCENDS
TROVE
VETTED
WARRANTS
WORSE

"Darkode" was an online forum where members could share ideas, advice, and knowledge. But it was also a place to buy, sell, or trade malware, stolen identity information, and other illegal data. The administrators of the site were extremely selective when accepting new members, thoroughly vetting each one to prevent access by law enforcement.

P	S	K	E	R	A	W	L	A	M	C	A	K	K	D	X	Z
R	T	R	I	E	V	O	R	T	I	C	R	H	E	M	A	M
I	N	E	E	D	O	O	D	F	G	D	A	T	C	M	D	U
M	E	R	I	V	U	S	I	L	I	V	A	S	O	P	D	R
E	M	A	P	C	R	L	D	S	E	T	J	L	M	A	I	O
S	T	W	G	E	O	E	M	N	I	R	U	O	B	S	T	F
N	C	T	D	R	R	A	S	L	E	F	R	O	A	S	I	X
E	I	F	P	C	N	P	I	R	R	C	I	T	T	W	O	W
Z	D	O	S	T	D	C	E	A	O	I	S	Q	A	O	N	S
O	N	S	L	O	A	B	E	T	G	W	D	N	X	R	U	E
D	I	E	M	F	K	F	V	T	R	A	I	E	A	D	M	I
E	W	A	R	R	A	N	T	S	R	A	C	A	K	R	O	Z
P	I	U	S	E	G	R	A	H	C	F	T	C	T	A	T	U
N	O	P	E	R	A	T	O	R	S	Y	I	O	Y	A	M	R
H	A	E	N	E	L	O	T	S	D	B	O	I	R	B	D	E
Z	E	C	R	U	O	S	E	R	I	B	N	G	D	S	E	C
F	M	K	L	N	D	E	T	T	E	V	S	T	D	U	Q	R

Still, the FBI managed to infiltrate the site, and, with the help of partners in 19 countries, collected evidence against Darkode users in an operation called Shrouded Horizon. The forum was ultimately shut down, and dozens of cybercriminals around the world were arrested.

Answers on page 174.

A $10 Million Hack

ADDITIONAL	DECADES	MEDIA
ARSENAL	ENTERPRISING	MILLION
BANKING	EVIDENCE	MONITOR
BOW	FOCUS	NETWORK
BYTE	FOOTPRINT	OVERSEAS
CASE	FROZEN	PINPOINTED
CLIENTS	FUNDS	SALVO
COMPROMISE	GROUP	TRANSFERRED
CORPORATE	HACKERS	VALID
COUPLE	ILLEGAL	VIRTUAL
COURIER	LAPTOP	

It may have been the first case of a bank robbery that didn't require a gun, mask, or threatening note. From June to October 1994, more than $10 million disappeared from the savings of corporate bank customers at a major U.S. institution when their accounts were hacked.

W	R	O	D	B	T	N	I	R	P	T	O	O	F	H	R	L
D	B	A	N	K	I	N	G	B	Y	T	E	R	C	E	L	C
Y	V	T	X	Y	N	N	W	T	S	E	O	F	I	Y	O	A
N	V	A	R	I	D	O	O	I	O	T	L	R	U	R	P	Y
E	E	S	L	A	B	E	O	I	I	L	U	P	P	N	B	H
Z	N	O	U	I	N	W	S	N	L	O	A	O	U	M	D	L
O	T	D	V	C	D	S	O	I	C	L	R	P	Q	O	A	S
R	E	E	V	L	O	M	F	Q	M	A	I	X	T	N	C	W
F	R	T	F	I	A	F	Z	E	T	O	A	M	O	O	Z	L
O	P	N	I	H	R	S	H	E	R	R	R	I	F	P	P	J
V	R	I	S	A	Z	T	C	S	S	R	T	P	U	W	A	N
E	I	O	E	C	G	A	U	E	T	I	E	O	M	I	U	E
R	S	P	D	K	S	D	N	A	D	N	R	D	D	O	B	T
S	I	N	A	E	W	A	C	D	L	G	E	E	C	S	C	W
E	N	I	C	R	L	Z	A	B	K	H	M	I	L	S	W	O
A	G	P	E	S	K	N	U	L	A	G	E	L	L	I	F	R
S	H	L	D	E	V	I	D	E	N	C	E	G	K	C	S	K

An FBI investigation revealed that some of the money had been routed to a bank in San Francisco, and when a woman named Ekaterina Korlokova attempted to withdraw funds, she was arrested. She led agents to the mastermind behind the plot, Russian computer hacker Vladimir Levin. The case was a wakeup call for the FBI, who soon began expanding their cybercrime techniques.

 Answers on page 174.

The Dixie Mafia

CITIZENS	INMATES	PENITENTIARY
CORRUPTION	KILLED	PLENTY
CROOKS	LAWLESS	RESIDENTS
DEMANDS	LAWYER	REVAMPED
DOING	MAJORITY	SAFEGUARD
DRUGS	MAYOR	SHIPMENTS
ENFORCEMENT	MONEY	THUGS
EXTORTION	MURDERER	TRIAL
GAMBLING	ORGANIZATION	UNABATED
ILLICIT	OVERTAKEN	WORD
INJURY	PARTNER	

In the 1980s, the sheriff's department in Biloxi, Mississippi, was headed by Leroy Hobbs, who frequently associated with the so-called Dixie Mafia, a criminal organization founded in the 1960s. Hobbs and the Dixie Mafia did everything from hide drug shipments to release dangerous criminals from prison, all for a price.

G	K	I	L	S	G	U	R	D	D	E	T	A	B	A	N	U
Y	T	N	E	L	P	P	C	I	T	I	Z	E	N	S	A	D
X	C	A	J	D	R	A	U	G	E	F	A	S	C	I	C	O
O	T	R	I	A	L	S	T	N	E	M	P	I	H	S	F	I
M	X	Y	T	I	C	I	L	L	I	A	O	H	M	T	S	N
P	E	N	I	T	E	N	T	I	A	R	Y	E	A	C	S	G
A	N	N	I	S	U	R	S	U	G	O	C	N	J	Z	E	G
F	O	N	O	J	D	G	O	A	L	M	S	F	O	R	L	A
S	I	X	P	I	U	N	N	Y	U	Z	E	O	R	E	W	M
S	T	K	I	H	T	I	A	R	A	O	T	R	I	V	A	B
K	P	N	T	N	Z	R	D	M	R	M	A	C	T	A	L	L
O	U	W	E	A	J	E	O	E	E	R	M	E	Y	M	O	I
O	R	M	T	D	R	U	N	T	E	D	N	M	Z	P	L	N
R	R	I	O	E	I	T	R	Y	X	D	I	E	F	E	E	G
C	O	I	R	N	R	S	W	Y	R	E	P	N	H	D	Y	D
N	C	S	J	A	E	A	E	O	V	E	R	T	A	K	E	N
A	M	U	P	G	L	Y	W	R	F	K	I	L	L	E	D	Q

But when the mafia entrusted their lawyer, Pete Halat, with some of their money, he spent it and then blamed it on his former law partner, Judge Vincent Sherry. Sherry and his wife were murdered, and it took the FBI eight years to bring Halat and his cohorts to justice. Meanwhile, the Biloxi sheriff's department was revamped, and Hobbs landed in prison for 20 years.

Answers on page 174.

Sergey Viktorovich Petrov

AERONAUTICAL	ENGINEERING	PRECARIOUS
CARDS	EXPENSES	PROXIMITY
CONFERENCE	FIGHTER	RADIO
CONTAINERS	GATHERING	REGULAR
CONTRACT	HELD	SOCIAL
DIAGRAMS	INDEX	TRANSLATED
DEPART	INDIVIDUAL	VALUE
DESIGN	LOCATION	VERBAL
DINNER	PAPERS	VICINITY
DOCTORAL	PAYMENT	WING
DRAWINGS	POLICY	

When Russian citizen Sergey Viktorovich Petrov met an engineer at a social gathering in New York City in 1970, he displayed an unusual interest in the engineer's work. An employee at Grumman Aerospace Corporation, the engineer revealed that his company was working on the F-14 fighter aircraft for the U.S. Navy, and Petrov was eager for more information.

L	D	O	C	T	O	R	A	L	D	E	S	I	G	N	D	P
A	W	T	R	A	P	E	D	Y	C	I	L	O	P	E	R	Y
X	O	D	S	T	N	E	M	Y	A	P	T	A	T	Q	E	G
G	I	A	E	R	O	N	A	U	T	I	C	A	L	L	T	N
P	D	M	A	D	E	R	H	E	Q	W	L	Z	I	A	H	I
R	A	C	M	G	N	N	A	U	V	S	I	T	N	I	G	R
E	R	J	N	D	G	R	I	L	N	I	Z	R	D	C	I	E
C	S	I	D	E	I	D	B	A	U	H	C	I	E	O	F	H
A	W	Y	R	C	N	N	R	V	T	G	L	I	X	S	P	T
R	D	C	A	N	E	T	N	I	E	N	E	A	N	M	L	A
I	I	P	W	E	E	K	F	E	H	L	O	R	B	I	R	G
O	A	A	I	R	R	H	C	A	R	D	S	C	S	R	T	P
U	G	P	N	E	I	E	T	C	A	R	T	N	O	C	E	Y
S	R	E	G	F	N	L	A	U	D	I	V	I	D	N	I	V
V	A	R	S	N	G	D	A	J	E	X	P	E	N	S	E	S
U	M	S	H	O	X	L	J	H	L	O	C	A	T	I	O	N
B	S	D	W	C	L	Y	Y	T	I	M	I	X	O	R	P	N

Over the next two years, the engineer supplied Petrov with classified data about the project. But unbeknownst to Petrov, the suspicious man had contacted the FBI almost immediately after their first meeting. On February 14, 1972, agents closed in on Petrov and arrested him for espionage, but all charges were dismissed after he agreed to return to the Soviet Union.

Answers on page 174.

Testerman and Lovett

AMMUNITION	IMPRISONMENT	PHASE
BASEMENT	INJURIES	PLEAS
BELL	INTERSTATE	PORCH
DESERT	IRON	POSSE
DRIVER	JURY	REVOLVER
EVENTS	LABOR	SERIOUS
FELONS	LATTER	SOLDIERS
FUGITIVES	LIFE	THIEVERY
HANDBAG	OUTSKIRTS	WARRANTS
HIGHWAY	OVERSEAS	WIDOW
IMPOSED	PETTY	

When James Edward Testerman and Charles Joseph Lovett decided to desert the U.S. Army in 1942, they did so in violent fashion. After beating the sergeant in charge unconscious, they made off with guns and ammunition and then stole a car. They made their way to Abingdon, Virginia, where FBI agents Hubert Treacy and Charles Tignor confronted them in a café.

Z	D	O	P	B	P	O	R	C	H	E	S	A	H	P	R	I
A	D	C	U	O	D	R	I	V	E	R	C	R	L	H	I	R
O	E	S	H	T	Q	Z	E	R	S	U	E	A	A	Y	N	O
P	S	Q	T	Y	S	V	F	E	S	V	B	N	T	T	T	N
R	E	D	S	N	E	K	V	E	O	O	D	T	D	H	E	R
S	R	G	E	N	A	I	I	L	R	B	E	I	E	I	R	I
A	T	E	T	P	T	R	V	R	A	P	M	O	S	E	S	S
E	X	S	O	I	U	E	R	G	T	P	S	M	O	V	T	Y
S	T	S	G	J	R	L	X	A	R	S	R	G	P	E	A	A
R	S	U	N	I	T	Y	D	I	W	Y	O	G	M	R	T	W
E	F	I	C	W	J	A	S	I	L	I	F	E	I	Y	E	H
V	W	I	D	O	W	O	T	S	O	L	D	I	E	R	S	G
O	A	M	M	U	N	I	T	I	O	N	X	J	U	R	Y	I
G	X	W	K	M	L	G	S	E	R	I	O	U	S	B	D	H
D	Z	D	E	L	L	A	T	T	E	R	A	T	L	L	E	B
N	Q	N	B	F	E	L	O	N	S	A	E	L	P	U	W	W
E	T	D	B	I	N	T	N	E	M	E	S	A	B	B	L	X

Suddenly, Lovett pulled a gun and shot at the agents multiple times, killing Treacy and seriously wounding Tignor. Testerman and Lovett took cover in a nearby house, but authorities soon captured the duo. They were found guilty of murder and sentenced to life in prison.

Answers on page 175.

John Elgin Johnson

ALIBI	GRANDIOSE	PROWLING
ANONYMITY	JUDICIAL	RECOGNITION
BANDIT	LARCENY	REHABILITATION
BURGLARY	LEGION	REVOLVER
CONFINEMENT	MARKET	SEPULCHER
COUP	OBSCURITY	SULLEN
DARKNESS	OFFICER	TERM
DEFY	OPERATION	THEFT
DEPARTMENT	OWNER	TUTELAGE
DUBIOUS	PENAL	ZENITH
FITTING	PROBATION	

By the time he was 21 years old, John Elgin Johnson had been sent to prison three times, eventually landing himself in Alcatraz. When he was freed at the age of 34, he almost immediately returned to his life of crime, stealing a car and murdering its owner. The FBI tracked him across the country to a Baltimore movie theater, where they attempted to apprehend him as he was in a phone booth.

P	P	X	S	U	O	I	B	U	D	N	O	I	G	E	L	R
U	C	X	R	E	C	O	G	N	I	T	I	O	N	Y	E	R
O	C	F	N	O	I	T	A	R	E	P	O	F	V	H	T	S
C	O	M	R	P	E	N	A	L	M	G	H	O	A	E	S	E
T	N	G	E	L	A	R	C	E	N	Y	B	B	K	E	S	R
O	F	N	H	D	E	F	Y	I	J	S	I	R	N	O	H	A
F	I	I	C	D	D	I	T	W	C	L	A	K	I	W	S	Q
F	N	L	L	C	E	T	L	U	I	M	R	D	Y	A	U	A
I	E	W	U	X	I	P	R	T	N	A	N	V	R	E	L	N
C	M	O	P	F	H	I	A	O	D	A	B	J	A	G	L	O
E	E	R	E	C	T	T	I	R	R	P	U	E	L	A	E	N
R	N	P	S	Y	I	T	I	G	T	D	T	V	G	L	N	Y
R	T	D	M	O	A	J	A	N	I	M	F	Y	R	E	S	M
Y	E	R	N	B	M	L	U	C	E	J	E	M	U	T	V	I
B	E	N	O	H	I	P	I	M	D	Z	H	N	B	U	E	T
T	E	R	W	B	B	A	N	D	I	T	T	B	T	T	K	Y
W	P	D	I	O	L	A	F	R	E	V	O	L	V	E	R	H

But Johnson pulled a gun and began shooting, mortally wounding Special Agent J. Brady Murphy. Three other agents shot at Johnson, killing the career criminal. Murphy's last words, before succumbing to his injuries, were "May God have mercy on his soul.

Answers on page 175.

The Case of the Hollow Nickel

APARTMENT	ENCODE	PERIOD
AREA	HAND	PHOTOGRAPH
BATTERIES	HOLLOW	PORTRAY
COINS	INVESTIGATION	PROPRIETORS
CODED	JINGLING	RECEIPT
CREW	MIDDLE	SCENE
CUSTOMER	MYSTERY	TINY
DEFECT	NEWSBOY	TOOL
DELIVERY	NICKEL	TYPEWRITER
DOLLAR	NOVELTY	ZONE
DOOR	PECULIAR	

In 1953, a delivery boy discovered a hollow nickel mixed in with his change. Inside, he found a tiny photo of a series of numbers. The FBI was called to investigate the strange find but were stumped.

Z	G	V	O	P	T	E	B	S	E	I	R	E	T	T	A	B
A	R	E	A	Y	D	N	K	Y	D	T	P	T	P	P	L	E
I	W	V	J	O	N	H	E	O	R	S	Z	E	R	T	R	T
S	V	E	C	U	O	E	O	M	N	E	C	O	C	E	P	T
E	R	N	R	L	I	R	N	I	T	U	V	E	N	I	O	D
C	E	O	L	C	T	F	O	E	L	R	F	I	E	E	E	D
U	D	O	T	R	A	C	Y	I	C	E	A	C	L	D	M	C
S	W	Y	E	E	G	F	A	R	D	S	E	P	O	E	J	W
T	R	V	G	T	I	R	I	E	E	R	W	C	A	C	D	F
O	Y	O	N	I	T	R	P	H	O	T	O	G	R	A	P	H
M	N	N	I	R	S	P	P	I	B	D	S	H	W	F	V	N
E	I	E	L	W	E	Z	Z	O	T	U	O	Y	A	O	H	I
R	T	W	G	E	V	C	W	O	R	Q	U	I	M	N	H	C
I	F	S	N	P	N	O	O	I	V	P	U	A	R	E	D	K
W	W	B	I	Y	I	L	N	O	V	E	L	T	Y	E	X	E
R	E	O	J	T	F	D	O	L	L	A	R	K	J	L	P	L
F	L	Y	M	I	D	D	L	E	Y	P	O	R	T	R	A	Y

They caught a break in 1957, when a former Soviet spy, Reino Hayhanen, defected to the U.S. Hayhanen not only helped agents break the hollow nickel code—a message created by a Soviet spy—but also led them to other Soviet spies working in the country, including Rudolph Abel. Abel was later returned to the Soviet Union in exchange for American pilot and Soviet prisoner Francis Gary Powers.

 Answers on page 175.

The Tokyo Rose

ALIASES	FORMER	PERSON
ANALYSIS	FOUGHT	PRESS
APPLICATION	GOVERNMENT	PROGRAM
ARMY	HARDSHIPS	PROPAGANDA
BROADCASTS	LOSS	RECORDS
CRIME	MERIT	SURRENDER
DEMORALIZE	MICROPHONE	TAINT
DEPORT	MILITARY	TRAITOR
DEVOTED	NOTORIOUS	TREASON
DUTIES	PARDONED	VETERANS
EXCLUSIVE	PERJURE	

During World War II, U.S. troops used the name "Tokyo Rose" to refer to any English-speaking woman broadcasting Japanese propaganda. But after the war, journalists homed in on one particular broadcaster, American-born Iva Toguri d'Aquino, dubbing her the "real" Tokyo Rose.

H	A	R	D	S	H	I	P	S	D	E	V	O	T	E	D	X
A	P	R	T	Q	M	F	O	P	E	R	J	U	R	E	Q	R
P	R	E	A	O	N	E	G	F	T	R	E	A	S	O	N	G
P	O	M	I	J	I	Q	R	A	G	V	P	U	P	E	O	P
L	P	R	N	L	Y	K	L	I	I	S	R	R	N	V	I	E
I	A	O	T	O	M	I	D	S	T	R	O	O	E	Z	D	R
C	G	F	G	S	A	E	U	S	E	G	H	R	D	J	U	S
A	A	E	V	S	N	L	A	N	R	P	N	E	V	V	T	O
T	N	U	E	O	C	C	D	A	O	M	P	K	E	K	I	N
I	D	S	D	X	D	E	M	R	E	O	B	T	X	Z	E	O
O	A	R	E	A	R	M	C	N	R	B	E	F	Q	Z	S	P
N	A	R	O	X	R	I	T	T	T	R	A	I	T	O	R	J
P	P	R	M	S	M	R	A	N	A	L	Y	S	I	S	N	O
R	B	Q	W	Y	U	C	K	N	Y	R	A	T	I	L	I	M
R	E	C	O	R	D	S	S	N	O	T	O	R	I	O	U	S
Y	S	S	E	R	P	T	H	G	U	O	F	Y	Q	D	O	L
O	O	V	E	Z	I	L	A	R	O	M	E	D	G	C	U	T

The publicity caught the attention of the FBI, who arrested d'Aquino in San Francisco in 1948. After a controversial trial, in which some witnesses would later say they'd been forced to lie, d'Aquino was found guilty and sentenced to ten years in prison. In 1977, she was pardoned by President Gerald Ford.

Answers on page 175.

United Airlines Flight 629

ABOARD	FINGERPRINT	PLANE
AIR	FLARE	POSSIBLE
BAGGAGE	FRAGMENTS	RECOVERED
BODIES	FUEL	RELATIVES
CARGO	JIGSAW	TEMPORARY
CONTROL	KILLED	TOWER
CRASH	LIASON	TRAGEDY
DISASTER	MORGUE	VICTIM
EFFECTS	NORMAL	WAYBILLS
EXPERTS	PERSONS	WRECKAGE
FILES	PIT	

On November 1, 1955, United Airlines flight 629, routinely flying from Denver to Portland, crashed only 11 minutes into its flight. All 44 people aboard were killed, including Daisie King, whose luggage seemed to be obliterated by the crash.

M	Y	R	S	L	L	I	B	Y	A	W	F	Y	L	W	S	R
E	R	E	N	Z	P	O	W	P	W	I	I	V	N	K	N	C
L	A	T	W	Y	D	E	G	A	R	T	N	A	Q	D	O	Z
B	R	S	F	I	L	E	S	S	E	U	G	R	O	M	S	G
I	O	A	E	P	S	T	R	E	P	X	E	C	E	B	R	F
S	P	S	C	K	M	Z	B	H	P	P	R	O	R	J	E	Z
S	M	I	S	R	O	I	C	S	L	R	P	N	H	I	P	D
O	E	D	L	E	A	M	L	J	A	L	R	T	N	D	A	R
P	T	L	Z	F	V	S	D	I	N	V	I	R	O	E	S	A
K	C	A	R	G	O	I	H	G	E	I	N	O	R	R	T	O
N	J	I	S	Y	X	M	T	S	X	G	T	L	M	E	N	B
O	R	H	W	T	D	E	G	A	G	G	A	B	A	V	E	A
S	F	K	E	E	C	B	F	W	L	Q	F	K	L	O	M	H
A	U	F	L	K	A	E	T	L	I	E	L	X	C	C	G	M
I	P	L	E	U	F	R	F	I	A	B	R	I	D	E	A	O
L	I	V	I	C	T	I	M	F	P	R	P	N	Q	R	R	U
K	R	E	W	O	T	W	G	J	E	X	E	Y	U	X	F	W

Investigators from the FBI contacted King's son, Jack Gilbert Graham, and during questioning discovered that the man had taken out life insurance and travel insurance policies on the life of his mother. After several interrogations, Graham confessed to hiding a timebomb in his mother's luggage, with the intention of collecting insurance money. He was found guilty of murder and was executed in 1957.

Answers on page 176.

The Medgar Evers Assassination

AGAINST	HEARD	RIPE
BOTH	JURY	SPEECH
BRAG	KILLED	STAGGERED
BRUTAL	MIDNIGHT	STORIES
COMMUNITY	MILITARY	SUBURBAN
DEATH	MOTIVE	TRIALS
EVIDENCE	OBVIOUS	VERDICT
EXPERTS	POLICE	WALK
FINGERPRINT	PROSECUTORS	WEAPON
FORMIDABLE	PROTESTS	WITNESSES
FREE	REVISIT	

Medgar Evers was a World War II veteran and civil rights leader who was senselessly murdered outside his own home on June 12, 1963. The FBI quickly found the rifle used to shoot Evers and identified his killer, a white supremacist named Byron De La Beckwith, from a fingerprint on the scope. But times were different, and an all-white jury allowed Beckwith to go free.

J	S	K	D	D	G	S	U	B	U	R	B	A	N	E	M	B
U	E	O	P	O	L	I	C	E	S	D	H	E	A	R	D	P
U	I	B	B	B	O	T	H	N	G	H	C	P	L	J	R	N
H	R	V	S	R	O	T	U	C	E	S	O	R	P	X	U	D
E	O	I	F	C	O	F	O	R	M	I	D	A	B	L	E	D
X	T	O	E	R	O	Q	T	B	O	T	U	Y	M	R	P	F
P	S	U	J	C	E	M	W	C	S	A	R	Y	E	A	I	R
E	G	S	K	R	N	E	M	N	I	I	O	G	Z	N	Y	W
R	M	W	V	I	A	E	I	U	P	D	G	A	G	T	R	A
T	I	I	P	P	L	A	D	E	N	A	R	E	F	H	A	L
S	D	T	O	R	G	L	V	I	T	I	R	E	F	C	T	K
B	N	N	N	A	F	I	E	S	V	P	T	N	V	E	I	T
R	I	E	R	G	T	C	F	D	R	E	V	Y	C	E	L	R
A	G	S	G	O	D	L	T	I	S	I	V	E	R	P	I	I
G	H	S	M	B	J	Z	N	L	A	T	U	R	B	S	M	A
H	T	E	W	Z	P	T	A	H	H	J	E	J	U	R	Y	L
M	N	S	T	S	E	T	O	R	P	N	H	T	A	E	D	S

In 1990, the case was reopened, this time with new evidence from witnesses who heard Beckwith confess to the crime. Finally, in 1994, 31 years after Evers' murder, Beckwith was rightfully convicted and sentenced to life in prison.

Answers on page 176.

The Melissa Virus

ATTACK	INFECTION	REMOVE
BAIT	INTERNET	SIGNIFICANT
CLEANUP	MACRO	SINISTER
COMPUTER	MILLION	STATE
CRAWL	MONEY	STEAL
CYBER	NETWORKS	STRIPPER
DANGER	ONLINE	SYSTEM
DEVIOUS	POTENT	VIRUSES
EMAIL	PRISON	WAVE
FEDERAL	PROGRAMMER	WEB
HIJACK	REALITY	

In March 1999, a New Jersey programmer named David Lee Smith posted a file in an internet group that promised free access to paid adult websites. In reality, the file unleashed a virus on the computers of users who clicked on it, in turn spreading the virus to their contacts. Within days, the Melissa Virus, which Smith reportedly named after a stripper, was wreaking havoc across the country.

D	G	S	H	O	O	E	S	C	N	S	E	S	U	R	I	V
S	H	U	Q	K	R	E	Z	O	S	Y	S	T	E	M	L	L
I	K	I	V	G	V	C	I	P	R	S	V	B	A	I	T	R
N	T	Y	J	O	B	T	A	E	P	N	Q	F	J	T	E	E
I	Z	S	M	A	C	C	T	M	C	O	A	E	S	G	S	M
S	T	E	T	E	C	U	Y	D	L	Y	T	D	I	U	I	M
T	R	N	F	R	P	K	E	T	E	I	R	E	Y	R	R	A
E	Z	N	A	M	I	V	Q	E	A	L	A	R	N	H	T	R
R	I	W	O	C	I	P	Q	N	N	W	B	A	X	T	N	G
E	A	C	F	O	I	D	P	R	U	A	S	L	A	O	O	O
A	E	C	U	R	O	F	L	E	P	R	Z	C	S	S	N	R
L	N	S	F	X	V	B	I	T	R	C	K	I	L	T	L	P
I	F	M	O	N	E	Y	Z	N	P	R	R	Z	L	E	I	X
T	T	R	E	G	N	A	D	I	G	P	E	X	D	A	N	W
Y	E	M	A	I	L	W	A	V	E	I	K	B	N	L	E	E
U	L	N	O	I	L	L	I	M	D	E	S	C	Y	O	S	B
P	U	N	E	T	W	O	R	K	S	H	N	J	H	C	D	F

The FBI sent out warnings to the public, and thanks to Smith's "electronic fingerprints" they had him in custody by April 1. The virus led to the creation of the FBI's Cyber Division, which works to protect America's electronic network.

Answers on page 176.

The Doll Woman

ALLEGATION	FRONT	RECEIVE
ANTIQUE	FURTHER	REGIONAL
AWFUL	HOBBYISTS	REJOIN
CENSORS	HOMES	SHIPYARD
CERTAIN	HULU	STEMMED
DAMAGED	HUSBAND	TRANSACTIONS
DAUGHTER	INTERCEPTED	TRANSMITTED
DEFENSE	KNOWN	TREMENDOUS
ENVELOPES	LETTER	WARSHIP
EXAMINATION	MATE	WEALTHY
FLEET	POSITION	

Velvalee Dickinson was born in California in 1893 and moved to New York City in 1937. There, she opened a doll shop that catered to wealthy collectors. But when the FBI was forwarded a series of strange letters in 1942, Dickinson was suspected of more than just selling dolls: she was selling secrets to the Japanese.

D	D	Z	I	T	T	E	O	D	W	N	S	D	D	D	H	D
E	R	D	C	I	D	R	A	L	O	E	A	E	E	V	N	Q
F	A	M	L	K	N	M	E	I	F	U	A	M	M	A	Z	R
E	Y	A	J	A	A	T	T	M	G	U	M	L	B	O	E	G
N	P	T	Y	G	N	A	E	H	E	E	R	S	T	T	H	C
S	I	E	E	G	N	O	T	R	T	N	U	T	T	H	T	E
E	H	D	Z	I	N	E	I	S	C	H	D	E	H	R	Y	N
B	S	A	M	G	R	G	Q	G	V	E	L	O	A	E	A	S
T	R	A	N	S	M	I	T	T	E	D	P	N	U	L	R	O
W	X	A	N	T	U	N	E	U	N	R	S	T	L	S	F	R
E	R	W	C	Q	I	E	W	O	A	A	X	E	E	R	O	S
V	E	A	X	P	L	Q	I	O	C	H	G	D	Z	D	L	X
I	J	R	A	F	H	T	U	T	N	A	T	N	O	R	F	V
E	O	S	P	W	I	D	I	E	T	K	Q	Y	H	U	L	U
C	I	H	P	S	F	O	A	I	N	I	A	T	R	E	C	F
E	N	I	O	O	N	U	O	S	T	S	I	Y	B	B	O	H
R	M	P	K	S	X	N	L	E	N	V	E	L	O	P	E	S

The letters used "dolls" as a code for U.S. Navy ships, and Dickinson would relay information about the location and status of these "dolls." An investigation revealed that Dickinson frequently hobnobbed with Japanese diplomats, and her typewriter was matched to the letters. She was arrested in 1944 and spent six years in prison.

Answers on page 176.

Vonsiatsky Espionage

ATTEND	DOCK	PROSECUTION
BACKGROUND	FASCISTS	RESULT
BROTHERHOOD	FICTITIOUS	REVOLUTIONARY
CASH	GERMAN	RING
CHARITY	LEADER	SENIOR
CHIEF	LEAFLETS	SOVIET
CITIZEN	MAJOR	STRUCTURE
COLONEL	NATURALIZED	SUBSEQUENT
CONFERENCE	OPPORTUNITY	SUMMER
CONSPIRACY	PASSAGE	TENSION
DISTRICT	PRIEST	

Anastase Vonsiatsky was born in Russia in 1898 but moved to the United States in 1921. A staunch critic of the communist regime in his homeland, he founded a fascist organization known as the All Russian National Revolutionary Party and set up its headquarters in Connecticut. To promote his cause, he traveled the world, rubbing elbows with leaders including a Japanese Army general and Adolph Hitler.

T	C	I	R	T	S	I	D	E	T	E	I	V	O	S	Q	A
N	X	M	A	J	O	R	L	R	R	E	S	U	L	T	T	M
O	R	W	R	L	B	P	V	U	S	M	L	D	G	T	J	Y
I	P	Y	O	C	R	A	N	T	T	P	O	E	E	A	T	F
T	S	C	I	G	O	S	F	C	C	C	R	N	A	I	N	G
U	T	A	N	E	T	S	E	U	K	A	D	I	R	D	N	N
C	E	R	E	R	H	A	I	R	J	W	S	A	E	I	E	B
E	L	I	S	M	E	G	H	T	Y	L	H	H	R	S	T	R
S	F	P	T	A	R	E	C	S	C	C	H	P	E	K	T	W
O	A	S	E	N	H	T	C	O	N	F	E	R	E	N	C	E
R	E	N	N	M	O	C	F	A	S	C	I	S	T	S	F	U
P	L	O	S	C	O	B	A	C	K	G	R	O	U	N	D	F
U	X	C	I	L	D	O	P	P	O	R	T	U	N	I	T	Y
Z	E	L	O	S	D	E	Z	I	L	A	R	U	T	A	N	V
Y	H	N	N	R	E	V	O	L	U	T	I	O	N	A	R	Y
N	E	Z	I	T	I	C	T	N	E	U	Q	E	S	B	U	S
L	S	U	M	M	E	R	F	I	C	T	I	T	I	O	U	S

By the 1940s, these activities caught the attention of the FBI, who discovered that Vonsiatsky, along with several co-conspirators, had aided a member of the German-American Bund. Agents discovered dozens of guns and swastika armbands at Vonsiatsky's Connecticut home, and he was arrested in 1942.

Answers on page 177.

Wall Street Bombing 1920

AFTERMATH	EVIDENCE	POLICE
ANARCHIST	EXPLOSION	PRINTING
ANIMAL	FIRE	RECOLLECTIONS
ATTACK	FLYERS	SUCCUMBED
AVIDLY	FOMENTED	TOLL
CANVAS	HORSE	TRACE
CARNAGE	INTENTIONAL	VAGUE
CART	KILLING	WAGON
CROWD	LIBRARY	WINDOWS
CRUCIAL	LUNCH	WORE
DILIGENTLY	OVERNIGHT	

At just after noon on September 16, 1920, a horse-drawn cart packed with a bomb exploded outside the J.P. Morgan building in New York City, killing 40 people and injuring hundreds. Resilient Wall Street was up and running again the next day, but the quick clean-up after the attack meant that vital evidence was no doubt lost.

O	V	E	R	N	I	G	H	T	C	R	U	C	I	A	L	R
F	G	N	I	T	N	I	R	P	T	R	A	C	H	K	T	L
D	A	N	A	R	C	H	I	S	T	Z	A	V	A	L	A	A
I	R	C	W	F	R	Q	L	U	N	C	H	F	I	N	M	B
L	E	C	I	L	O	P	T	O	L	L	T	B	O	F	S	R
I	I	Q	N	Y	L	X	X	V	E	E	R	I	Q	U	X	E
G	B	A	D	E	V	Y	M	X	R	A	T	S	C	W	C	C
E	E	H	O	R	S	E	P	M	R	N	S	C	Z	R	S	O
N	G	P	W	S	K	L	A	Y	E	I	U	U	O	E	A	L
T	W	A	S	U	O	T	F	T	V	M	E	W	H	C	V	L
L	A	B	N	S	H	O	N	A	B	A	D	L	Y	N	N	E
Y	G	R	I	R	M	I	G	E	T	L	O	L	O	E	A	C
E	O	O	E	E	A	U	D	T	B	T	D	P	M	D	C	T
A	N	H	N	J	E	C	W	Y	R	I	A	R	R	I	M	I
S	V	T	W	D	B	Y	Q	O	V	A	V	C	W	V	W	O
D	E	F	I	R	E	A	I	A	R	U	C	I	K	E	A	N
D	R	G	N	I	L	L	I	K	F	E	D	E	V	U	O	S

The FBI's predecessor, the Bureau of Investigation, did their best to identify the culprits responsible for the explosion, narrowing their suspects down to a group of Italian anarchists. Unfortunately, they were never able to definitively pinpoint the terrorists, and the identity of the bomber has remained a mystery.

Answers on page 177.

ABSCAM

BOGUS	FAKE	PEDDLING
BONDS	FRAUDULENT	POLITICIANS
BRIBE	GAMBLING	PUBLIC
BUSINESS	GUILTY	RIVETING
CASE	HOCKING	SAFEGUARDS
CONVICTED	IMPORTANCE	SENATOR
CORRUPT	INTEREST	SHEIK
DOZEN	INVESTIGATION	STING
DUST	LICENSE	UNFOLDING
ENTRAPMENT	OPERATION	WORK
ENVELOPE	PAINTINGS	

In July 1978, the FBI set up an undercover operation to recover stolen art. Posing as representatives of a fictitious Middle Eastern sheik, agents set up a fake company called "Abdul Enterprises" and found art thieves who were willing to sell stolen art to the wealthy "sheik." The successful operation not only helped the FBI recover millions in stolen artwork, but led them to other criminals, as well.

E	D	S	Q	B	O	G	U	S	R	O	T	A	N	E	S	I
C	S	E	T	N	E	L	U	D	U	A	R	F	S	V	G	N
N	O	H	T	S	E	R	E	T	N	I	D	S	G	N	R	V
A	U	W	E	C	P	X	V	Q	B	O	E	N	I	G	E	E
T	V	E	X	I	I	A	S	T	Z	N	I	T	N	S	B	S
R	N	S	C	F	K	V	Q	E	I	K	E	I	N	S	D	T
O	O	A	S	A	J	F	N	S	C	V	T	E	O	D	E	I
P	I	C	G	E	K	J	U	O	I	S	C	O	K	R	L	G
M	T	E	N	N	Y	B	H	R	C	I	W	K	A	A	J	A
I	A	P	I	T	P	E	D	D	L	I	N	G	E	U	F	T
W	R	O	T	R	T	P	U	R	R	O	C	M	X	G	I	I
O	E	L	N	A	B	G	A	M	B	L	I	N	G	E	G	O
R	P	E	I	P	M	R	T	P	U	B	L	I	C	F	U	N
K	O	V	A	M	G	N	I	D	L	O	F	N	U	A	I	E
G	N	N	P	E	B	Z	W	B	U	N	F	G	S	S	L	M
W	B	E	K	N	S	U	M	T	E	D	Z	B	J	Q	T	E
P	O	L	I	T	I	C	I	A	N	S	D	U	S	T	Y	I

They even arrested more than a dozen U.S. government officials who were stuffing their pockets with bribe money. The investigation, which relied on the "scam" of "Abdul Enterprises," was famously code-named ABSCAM.

Answers on page 177.

Escape from Alcatraz

ALCATRAZ	INTENSIVE	RELATIVES
ALREADY	IRON	ROUGH
ATTEMPT	ITEMS	RUBBER
CAUGHT	LONELY	RULES
COLD	MAXIMUM	SECURITY
CONVICTS	ODD	STRICT
DUMMIES	PACIFIC	TOUGHER
FOOL	PHOTO	TUBE
FORBIDDING	PLACE	VEST
GUARD	PLASTER	WATER
INMATES	PRISON	

On June 12, 1962, prisoners John Anglin, his brother Clarence, and Frank Morris escaped from Alcatraz Island, which was considered the world's most secure prison. When the FBI was called to investigate, they discovered that the prisoners had spent months secretly fashioning a raft out of raincoats, then climbed to the roof and shimmied down pipes to escape.

U	R	L	H	K	L	E	Z	A	R	T	A	C	L	A	W	L
T	C	I	R	T	S	B	H	T	D	V	N	X	Y	R	C	B
K	P	F	Q	N	A	U	L	S	H	C	T	P	R	O	C	L
Z	S	E	L	U	R	T	E	H	O	G	N	D	N	E	R	Y
J	F	V	D	D	O	V	Z	Q	L	U	U	V	I	V	A	I
I	E	O	S	C	I	F	I	C	A	P	I	A	D	I	L	R
T	S	B	O	T	Y	A	N	P	O	C	K	S	C	S	R	O
E	R	T	A	L	W	F	I	M	T	T	Y	W	O	N	E	N
M	M	L	T	A	D	R	O	S	A	T	O	C	L	E	A	N
S	E	Y	T	P	E	U	Y	R	U	X	I	H	G	T	D	M
R	P	E	T	H	M	K	M	R	B	N	I	M	P	N	Y	Y
U	R	R	G	I	R	E	E	M	M	I	H	M	W	I	D	L
O	D	U	I	U	R	T	T	A	I	G	D	G	U	L	R	E
M	O	T	B	S	S	U	T	T	U	E	Z	D	O	M	A	N
T	C	B	S	A	O	E	C	O	A	I	S	C	I	W	U	O
N	E	B	L	E	S	N	R	E	Z	S	N	N	F	N	G	L
R	P	P	F	U	V	D	R	R	S	P	L	A	C	E	G	W

While they did successfully leave the island, no one knows if they survived the chilly waters of the Pacific long enough to make it to land. The FBI never found evidence that the trio lived, and officially closed the case in 1979.

Answers on page 177.

Bank Heist in Indiana

ACCESS	DEATH	OVER
ACTIVITY	DELINQUENT	PAROLED
ADVISED	ESCAPE	PETTY
APPREHENDED	FELONY	SENTENCE
BANK	GUILTY	STATE
CASHIER	INDICTMENT	SUM
CHARGE	INTERROGATION	TORCH
CLEMENCY	LARCENY	VARIETIES
COMMIT	LOOT	VEHICLE
CONVICT	MOTOR	VICINITY
CUSTODY	NIGHT	

On the night of December 2, 1937, the State Bank of Lapel in Lapel, Indiana, was burglarized. An FBI investigation immediately flagged Joseph Earlywine, Fred Steffler, and William Hulett as suspects. Agents found Earlywine and Hulett on a farm in Illinois, where Hulett was easily arrested. Earlywine, however, put up a fight, shooting and mortally wounding Special Agent William Ramsey.

D	C	F	O	Z	D	H	U	W	D	K	E	D	A	N	S	E
I	U	S	H	C	R	O	T	E	T	C	V	I	E	I	E	L
M	S	S	E	C	C	A	L	Z	O	K	N	M	G	A	I	C
U	T	R	E	V	O	I	V	M	L	D	R	A	P	A	T	I
S	O	A	G	E	N	E	M	Y	I	E	P	A	L	D	E	H
M	D	L	F	Q	T	I	N	C	I	P	R	O	W	V	I	E
A	Y	Y	U	A	T	O	T	H	R	O	O	A	A	I	R	V
P	W	E	T	X	L	M	S	E	L	T	C	J	E	S	A	S
O	N	S	I	E	E	A	H	E	E	S	C	A	P	E	V	E
T	B	X	F	N	C	E	D	G	M	O	T	O	R	D	O	N
I	Y	A	T	A	N	A	C	T	I	V	I	T	Y	L	C	T
L	F	I	N	D	Z	K	Y	T	L	I	U	G	N	R	E	E
V	W	A	E	K	Y	T	I	N	I	C	I	V	I	I	G	N
L	F	D	Y	C	N	E	M	E	L	C	F	S	G	C	R	C
N	O	I	T	A	G	O	R	R	E	T	N	I	H	P	A	E
K	P	Y	N	E	C	R	A	L	C	B	O	Z	T	P	H	D
P	P	E	T	T	Y	M	V	C	O	N	V	I	C	T	C	Z

Ramsey was able to return fire before succumbing to his injuries, hitting Earlywine in the forehead and killing him instantly. Steffler was later apprehended outside his home, and confessed to several burglaries. He was sentenced to 15 years in prison, but due to lack of evidence, Hulett was not prosecuted.

Answers on page 178.

Aldrich Ames

AGENTS	FEDERAL	PLEAS
AIDED	IDENTITIES	PURSUANT
ARRESTED	INCARCERATION	RUSSIANS
ASSIGNMENT	INTELLIGENCE	SECRETLY
AUTHORITIES	JUSTICE	SPYING
CHARGES	MEETINGS	SYSTEM
DEBRIEFED	MONTHS	TARGETED
DIPLOMAT	OCTOBER	TRAVEL
DOCUMENTS	OFFICERS	VETERAN
ESPIONAGE	OPERATIONS	VOLUNTEER
EXECUTED	OVERSEAS	

In May 1993, the FBI and CIA learned that many of their spies in Russia were being arrested and executed, their covert lives obviously uncovered. When the FBI began investigating the situation, they discovered that a CIA agent named Aldrich Ames had seemingly stumbled into a large amount of money—almost $2 million, in fact.

E	O	J	R	I	N	T	E	L	L	I	G	E	N	C	E	S
G	E	W	M	N	T	N	A	U	S	R	U	P	P	D	S	N
A	S	P	Y	I	N	G	D	E	F	E	I	R	B	E	D	O
N	S	A	E	S	R	E	V	O	A	L	G	Z	I	G	O	I
O	R	B	S	H	T	N	O	M	S	D	U	R	T	X	F	T
I	A	R	R	E	S	T	E	D	S	O	M	L	A	Z	F	A
P	S	J	J	X	V	S	R	E	I	C	E	A	R	H	I	R
S	I	L	P	S	O	E	K	I	G	U	E	R	G	D	C	E
E	D	H	L	E	L	I	I	N	N	M	T	E	E	M	E	P
S	E	X	E	C	U	T	E	D	M	E	I	D	T	E	R	O
N	N	V	A	R	N	I	V	G	E	N	N	E	E	T	S	J
A	T	E	S	E	T	R	R	V	N	T	G	F	D	S	T	U
I	I	T	T	T	E	O	R	F	T	S	S	P	B	Y	R	S
S	T	E	Y	L	E	H	R	E	B	O	T	C	O	S	A	T
S	I	R	H	Y	R	T	X	K	S	T	N	E	G	A	V	I
U	E	A	T	T	O	U	D	I	P	L	O	M	A	T	E	C
R	S	N	O	I	T	A	R	E	C	R	A	C	N	I	L	E

They soon learned that Ames had volunteered his services to the KGB in 1985 and had secretly been passing along classified information for years. He was arrested and found guilty of espionage, and sentenced to life in prison without possibility of parole.

Answers on page 178.

The Murder of Judge Vance

ANALYZE	FEDERAL	PERSONAL
ANIMUS	HOLIDAYS	RESENTMENT
AUTHORIZED	HURT	SCENARIO
BOMB	INTERCEPTED	SERIAL
CHARGES	JUDGES	SOLID
CLEAR	LINKED	SPITEFUL
CONTACTS	MOTIVE	SUSPECTS
COURTHOUSE	NAME	SYSTEM
EVENTS	PACKAGE	TRAIL
EXPLODED	PARCEL	VICTIM
EXTENSIVE	PATTERN	

When a package showed up at the home of Robert Vance on December 16, 1989, the federal appeals judge assumed it was a Christmas gift. But when he opened it, a bomb exploded, killing him and injuring his wife. Three more bombs appeared over the next few days, one killing attorney Robert Robertson.

D	Q	L	I	N	K	E	D	M	O	T	I	V	E	W	N	K
D	E	T	P	E	C	R	E	T	N	I	K	O	U	A	U	S
P	X	R	C	E	E	G	A	K	C	A	P	P	M	P	R	E
A	P	E	C	C	X	L	B	S	U	S	P	E	C	T	S	G
R	S	X	O	S	A	T	M	T	A	D	Z	A	R	S	M	R
C	R	P	U	Y	N	E	E	V	N	Y	Q	E	S	E	I	A
E	T	L	R	A	I	Z	U	N	L	R	S	G	T	G	T	H
L	R	O	T	D	M	I	F	A	S	E	E	F	C	D	C	C
N	A	D	H	I	U	B	N	L	N	I	S	T	A	U	I	E
Q	I	E	O	L	S	A	O	T	U	E	V	F	T	J	V	S
M	L	D	U	O	V	I	M	M	R	F	F	E	N	A	I	O
E	J	G	S	H	R	E	W	I	B	Z	E	J	O	V	P	L
T	C	U	E	A	N	H	A	L	W	T	R	T	C	X	M	I
S	X	L	N	T	L	L	A	U	T	H	O	R	I	Z	E	D
Y	M	E	E	S	T	N	E	V	E	Z	S	G	N	P	N	A
S	C	A	L	A	R	E	D	E	F	E	Y	M	B	F	S	F
S	H	U	R	T	R	T	K	L	A	N	O	S	R	E	P	A

The FBI called in a bomb expert, who recognized the bombs as the work of a man named Walter Moody. Moody had been convicted of bomb possession 17 years earlier, and harbored a deep hatred of the justice system, prompting him to send the bombs. He was convicted of murder and executed in 2018.

Answers on page 178.

Theft of the Krupp Diamond

ALLEGED	EITHER	MONEY
APPEAL	FORCED	RANCH
ATTRACTIVE	FOREMAN	RAP
AUCTION	FORTUNE	RING
BAGUETTE	FUGITIVE	RUMOR
BARONESS	GROCER	SPRAWLING
BLAME	GUILTY	THIEVES
BLOOD	HOMEWORK	TRANSPORTED
CAMERA	JEWELER	WEALTHY
COUNTRY	LOVED	ZIGZAG
DINNER	MASTERMIND	

On the evening of April 10, 1959, thieves broke into the Las Vegas home of a wealthy woman named Vera Krupp and stole her most prized possession: a 33-carat diamond ring. The FBI soon focused on a fugitive named John Hagenson, who was wanted for a similar crime in California. They tracked Hagenson across the country, arresting him in Louisiana.

L	D	N	O	I	T	C	U	A	T	Z	H	K	A	P	N	S
E	V	I	T	I	G	U	F	F	C	C	I	M	L	L	O	V
F	B	A	R	O	N	E	S	S	O	T	Q	B	O	A	D	D
O	T	G	R	O	C	E	R	Z	D	R	A	L	V	E	N	A
R	R	Z	T	H	I	E	V	E	S	G	T	J	E	P	I	D
E	A	I	T	G	V	Y	G	Y	U	F	E	U	D	P	M	A
M	N	G	O	U	E	E	E	E	H	W	D	E	N	A	R	W
A	S	Z	T	I	L	V	T	N	E	T	I	Y	K	E	E	C
N	P	A	K	L	B	T	I	L	O	T	L	R	M	H	T	Y
T	O	G	A	T	E	L	E	T	H	M	O	A	X	W	S	R
K	R	A	P	Y	X	R	O	E	C	W	C	X	E	G	A	T
R	T	K	L	P	B	F	R	O	E	A	R	R	A	W	M	N
A	E	R	W	J	L	T	K	M	D	Q	R	I	L	U	R	U
Z	D	N	J	D	A	F	O	R	C	E	D	T	N	A	O	O
K	E	V	N	O	M	H	K	P	S	W	R	S	T	G	M	C
E	O	M	V	I	E	K	M	H	C	N	A	R	O	A	U	T
R	Z	A	R	B	D	G	N	I	L	W	A	R	P	S	R	H

Hagenson led the FBI to other suspects, including James Reves, who had hidden the diamond ring in a hotel room in New Jersey. After Krupp's death in 1968, the impressive ring was auctioned off, becoming the possession of none other than Elizabeth Taylor.

Answers on page 178.

MIBURN

ACTIVE	DOZEN	MURDEROUS
ANNIVERSARY	DROVE	NEVER
BIASED	HOLLOWS	NOTIFY
BODIES	HOMICIDAL	PREACHER
BOYCOTT	IMPETUS	SWAMPS
CAMPAIGN	INFILTRATE	TARGET
CHURCH	INTERVIEWS	TELEPHONE
COMPREHENSIVE	INTIMIDATION	VOTER
CONVICTED	LANDMARK	WAGON
CRIMES	LAUNCHED	WITNESSES
DEPARTMENT	MASSIVE	

When three young men (Michael Schwerner, James Chaney, and Andrew Goodman) went missing near Philadelphia, Mississippi, in June 1964, the FBI suspected foul play. The men had been working to register blacks to vote, despite intimidation and threats from the KKK.

D	E	H	C	N	U	A	L	S	E	S	S	E	N	T	I	W
J	R	L	K	T	Z	U	C	I	N	D	C	W	K	U	M	F
L	Y	F	I	T	O	N	O	N	O	C	H	U	R	C	H	E
W	Z	H	W	O	P	I	M	T	I	R	O	K	A	H	T	V
Y	O	Q	F	C	R	M	P	E	T	E	M	C	M	S	N	I
D	R	J	Y	Y	E	P	R	R	A	V	I	O	D	U	E	S
U	V	A	Q	O	A	E	E	V	D	E	C	N	N	O	M	S
H	D	O	S	B	C	T	H	I	I	N	I	V	A	R	T	A
C	O	E	T	R	H	U	E	E	M	E	D	I	L	E	R	M
S	R	L	S	E	E	S	N	W	I	V	A	C	D	D	A	E
W	W	I	L	A	R	V	S	S	T	I	L	T	O	R	P	V
A	A	N	M	O	I	X	I	H	N	T	C	E	Z	U	E	O
M	G	D	B	E	W	B	V	N	I	C	O	D	E	M	D	R
P	O	W	K	S	S	S	E	W	N	A	R	V	N	H	Q	D
S	N	N	G	I	A	P	M	A	C	A	B	O	D	I	E	S
J	T	E	G	R	A	T	D	T	E	L	E	P	H	O	N	E
D	G	Z	E	T	A	R	T	L	I	F	N	I	V	E	N	T

Two days after the disappearance, the men's burned-out car was found, leading the FBI to name the case Mississippi Burning. Sadly, the bodies of the men were found in August, buried on a farm. Seven people were convicted, although none on murder charges. But the case united the nation in its determination to pass the Civil Rights Act of 1964.

Answers on page 179.

Congressman Jefferson

ACTIVITY	DELEGATIONS	OWNERSHIP
AGENCIES	DENIED	PETITION
APPROVAL	DOCUMENTS	RECORDER
BRIBES	ENFORCEMENT	RESIDENCE
BUNDLE	EXCHANGE	SOLICIT
CAMERA	FINANCIAL	STAFFERS
CASH	FREEZER	SURVEILLANCE
CAUGHT	ILLEGAL	TRIAL
CONGRESS	LETTERHEAD	VALUABLE
CORRUPT	MEMBER	WITNESS
CRIME	OFFICIAL	

In 2005, a Virginia businesswoman contacted the FBI with information concerning a member of the U.S. Congress. The congressman, William Jefferson, had offered to aid her business in exchange for a percentage of ownership in her company. She agreed to assist the FBI in their investigation of Jefferson, wearing a body recorder during their meetings.

R	E	S	I	D	E	N	C	E	T	P	U	R	R	O	C	G
S	U	R	V	E	I	L	L	A	N	C	E	P	Q	S	D	L
S	I	M	E	M	B	E	R	Z	S	P	I	O	C	S	W	A
E	X	C	H	A	N	G	E	H	K	H	A	H	D	E	R	I
N	L	A	V	O	R	P	P	A	S	G	L	G	E	R	E	R
T	R	E	C	O	R	D	E	R	S	A	Y	S	N	G	Z	T
I	E	N	M	V	K	O	E	C	I	E	T	U	I	N	E	O
W	I	F	G	K	P	N	R	C	T	K	I	M	E	O	E	F
C	S	O	V	E	W	I	N	H	B	A	V	C	D	C	R	F
A	T	R	S	O	M	A	G	R	N	F	I	K	N	Y	F	I
M	N	C	T	E	N	U	I	N	O	I	T	I	T	E	P	C
E	E	E	A	I	A	B	S	O	L	I	C	I	T	I	G	I
R	M	M	F	C	E	W	E	E	L	B	A	U	L	A	V	A
A	U	E	F	S	F	N	D	A	E	H	R	E	T	T	E	L
D	C	N	E	L	A	G	E	L	L	I	H	J	P	C	Q	R
P	O	T	R	W	D	E	L	E	G	A	T	I	O	N	S	R
X	D	B	S	R	B	U	N	D	L	E	A	H	C	J	M	R

It was discovered that the congressman was soliciting bribes from other companies, as well as paying bribes to foreign officials, and a raid on his house turned up $90,000 hidden in a freezer. Jefferson was convicted of corruption in 2009 and sentenced to 13 years in federal prison

Answers on page 179.

The 1993 WTC Bombing

BAND	ERUPTION	RUBBLE
BANG	EXPLOSION	SCURRIED
BUILDING	FORCE	SINISTER
CELL	FUNDAMENTALIST	TASK
CONNECTIONS	INTERNATIONAL	TEAM
CONVICTED	KILLED	THUNDEROUS
CRUSHED	LANDMARKS	UNCOVERED
CYANIDE	MANHATTAN	VAN
DEADLY	OFFICE	VISION
DEPOSIT	PLAZA	WAREHOUSE
EPICENTER	REVERBERATE	

At just after noon on February 26, 1993, an explosion tore a 100-foot crater in the parking garage of the World Trade Center, killing six people and injuring more than a thousand. The FBI suspected terrorism and launched a massive investigation, encompassing 700 agents worldwide.

M	C	U	T	S	F	C	F	R	E	T	S	I	N	I	S	E
E	A	Q	E	S	U	L	E	X	P	L	O	S	I	O	N	C
G	S	J	A	R	N	O	O	R	C	V	A	U	D	E	B	I
N	N	U	M	U	D	O	C	D	A	Y	C	Z	P	A	L	F
A	M	Y	O	E	A	M	I	N	E	T	A	I	A	A	Z	F
B	I	E	I	H	M	N	M	T	A	L	C	N	N	L	G	O
E	S	D	O	D	E	T	O	S	C	E	L	O	I	B	P	C
T	K	E	J	E	N	R	K	I	N	E	I	I	U	D	O	S
A	R	R	D	A	T	P	A	T	T	T	N	I	K	N	E	C
R	A	E	E	D	A	Z	E	W	A	P	L	N	V	F	L	U
E	M	V	P	L	L	R	M	N	N	D	U	I	O	L	Q	R
B	D	O	O	Y	I	F	R	O	I	L	C	R	E	C	T	R
R	N	C	S	U	S	E	I	N	H	T	C	C	E	E	M	I
E	A	N	I	X	T	S	G	Z	E	E	L	B	B	U	R	E
V	L	U	T	N	I	M	O	D	C	R	U	S	H	E	D	D
E	C	Y	I	V	J	F	P	N	A	T	T	A	H	N	A	M
R	S	U	O	R	E	D	N	U	H	T	T	B	A	N	D	S

A vehicle identification number found in the rubble led them to several culprits, as well as a storage locker containing chemicals and cyanide gas. The mastermind of the bombing, Ramzi Yousef, was arrested in 1995, and the investigation also led to the discovery of a terrorist cell in Queens. Sadly, Yousef's uncle, Khalid Sheikh Mohammed, would later organize the 9/11 attacks.

Answers on page 179.

1985: Year of the Spy

AFFILIATES	EQUIPMENT	POLYGRAPH
ALONE	FATE	PRISON
ARRESTS	GASPS	RADIO
CLASSIFIED	GOVERNMENT	REVEALED
CONFEDERATE	LANGUAGE	ROUTINE
CRYPTOGRAPHIC	LIFE	SECRETS
DECADE	MILITARY	SPECIALIST
DEFECTOR	MOLES	SPIES
DETAILS	NATION	STRING
DEVASTATING	PASSED	TRIAL
DOZENS	PLED	

The FBI had their work cut out for them in 1985, when a string of espionage arrests revealed just how many moles were working in the U.S. government. Those arrested included U.S. Navy Warrant Officer John Anthony Walker Jr., who passed classified information to the Soviets for

C	G	C	D	K	C	O	N	F	E	D	E	R	A	T	E	B
M	N	M	I	A	S	A	S	A	S	B	I	B	C	D	A	N
T	X	C	L	H	J	P	Y	E	R	P	D	E	E	R	K	A
S	T	O	J	D	P	O	E	O	I	E	S	V	I	O	A	T
N	N	L	N	Y	I	A	U	C	L	P	A	A	U	T	F	I
E	E	W	A	D	R	T	R	A	I	S	S	E	G	C	F	O
Z	M	L	A	N	I	A	E	G	T	A	Q	S	I	E	I	N
O	N	R	I	N	G	V	T	A	O	U	L	D	M	F	L	H
D	R	P	E	F	E	U	T	I	I	T	E	I	T	E	I	P
S	E	S	X	R	E	I	A	P	L	S	P	R	S	D	A	O
L	V	E	Z	S	N	S	M	G	S	I	I	Y	U	T	T	L
I	O	L	Q	G	T	E	J	A	E	A	M	F	R	J	E	Y
A	G	O	G	S	N	A	P	X	L	U	F	K	H	C	S	G
T	H	M	E	T	B	S	T	E	R	C	E	S	V	M	P	R
E	O	R	Q	D	E	I	F	I	S	S	A	L	C	L	L	A
D	R	S	T	R	I	N	G	E	D	A	C	E	D	B	E	P
A	W	R	E	T	A	F	N	O	S	I	R	P	D	H	D	H

seventeen years; CIA clerk Sharon Marie Scranage, who provided information to the Ghanaian head of state in 1983; and CIA translator Larry Wu-tai Chin, who gave China decades of classified documents and photographs. Dozens of other spies were also identified and arrested, prompting the media to dub 1985 the "Year of the Spy."

 Answers on page 179.

Alger Hiss

ACCESS	GOVERNMENT	PERJURY
AFTERMATH	GUILTY	POWER
CENTRAL	ISSUE	PRODDED
COMMUNISM	JURY	SECRETS
CORROBORATE	JUSTICE	SENTENCED
CREATE	LAWYER	SOVIETS
DELIBERATIONS	LYING	TESTIMONY
DOCUMENTS	MAGAZINE	TRIAL
DOZENS	PACKAGE	UNDERGROUND
EDITOR	PARTISAN	VERDICT
ESPIONAGE	PENETRATION	

In a case of he said/he said, Whittaker Chambers, an editor at *Time* magazine, accused Alger Hiss, a government lawyer and state department official, of espionage during testimony to the House Committee on Un-American Activities in 1948. Hiss denied the accusation under oath, not once, but twice, even suing Chambers for libel.

G	O	V	E	R	N	M	E	N	T	Z	R	S	P	J	S	K
N	B	A	B	E	R	S	S	E	C	C	A	T	A	P	E	N
I	I	Y	D	E	T	G	K	N	I	W	G	N	C	E	N	O
Y	H	R	W	E	U	A	A	S	H	S	M	E	K	R	T	I
L	G	O	E	I	L	S	R	T	N	G	S	M	A	J	E	T
C	P	E	L	S	I	I	A	O	L	E	D	U	G	U	N	A
Q	O	T	N	T	P	M	B	E	B	N	Z	C	E	R	C	R
H	Y	M	R	I	R	I	D	E	U	O	N	O	H	Y	E	T
K	T	A	M	E	Z	I	O	O	R	O	R	D	D	L	D	E
L	P	C	T	U	T	A	R	N	S	A	E	R	A	D	E	N
A	L	F	I	O	N	G	G	O	A	D	T	W	O	T	V	E
R	A	A	R	D	R	I	V	A	D	G	Y	I	A	C	N	P
T	J	E	I	E	R	I	S	O	M	E	E	E	O	A	N	C
N	F	U	D	R	E	E	R	M	R	U	R	D	D	N	B	J
E	Q	N	R	T	T	P	V	B	N	C	D	I	K	D	S	A
C	U	P	S	Y	Y	N	O	M	I	T	S	E	T	E	W	P
S	T	E	R	C	E	S	G	B	J	U	S	T	I	C	E	T

But when Chambers produced proof of Hiss's espionage, including documents he had hidden inside a pumpkin on his farm—now known as the "Pumpkin Papers"—the jig was up. While the statute of limitations prevented an espionage charge, Hiss was found guilty of two counts of perjury and sentenced to five years in prison.

The Rosenbergs

ATOMIC	ENLISTED	MATERIAL
BOMB	ESPIONAGE	MEMBERS
CENSUS	FEDERAL	NATION
CHEMIST	FOREIGN	NETWORK
COLLEGE	IDENTITY	PANACEA
CONSPIRACY	INCIDENT	PETITION
CONTACT	INDICTMENT	PLEA
CUSTODY	INGENUITY	PRINCIPLES
DEFAULT	LITERATURE	PRONOUNCE
DETONATION	MACHINE	PUBLIC
DISCOVERY	MANUFACTURING	

Julius Rosenberg and Ethel Greenglass were both the children of Russian immigrants and grew up in New York City. In 1939, after Julius earned a degree in electrical engineering, the pair married and eventually had two children. But their all-American lifestyle concealed a secret: the Rosenbergs, along with a network of acquaintances that included Ethel's brother, David, were spies for the Communist Party.

K	E	G	E	L	L	O	C	F	E	D	E	R	A	L	A	G
M	Y	P	A	N	A	C	E	A	E	N	L	I	S	T	E	D
Q	D	E	K	N	Z	P	R	O	N	O	U	N	C	E	L	M
H	O	G	N	I	R	U	T	C	A	F	U	N	A	M	P	D
H	T	M	O	C	P	T	L	U	A	F	E	D	J	X	U	U
D	S	N	N	G	I	E	R	O	F	C	I	M	O	T	A	N
I	U	J	R	E	R	U	T	A	R	E	T	I	L	D	M	I
S	C	Y	P	R	I	N	C	I	P	L	E	S	E	F	A	N
C	Y	A	C	Q	T	K	E	B	T	J	Q	T	V	Y	T	D
O	T	S	G	A	R	C	M	S	C	I	O	L	T	S	E	I
V	I	B	R	O	R	M	A	H	P	N	O	I	N	U	R	C
E	U	P	W	E	A	I	E	T	A	I	T	N	O	S	I	T
R	N	T	U	C	B	M	P	T	N	N	O	G	I	N	A	M
Y	E	U	H	B	I	M	I	S	E	O	P	N	T	E	L	E
N	G	I	A	S	L	O	E	D	N	V	C	W	A	C	S	N
L	N	S	T	D	N	I	I	M	B	O	M	B	N	G	B	T
E	I	T	N	E	D	I	C	N	I	D	C	M	R	A	E	U

Due to the couple's orchestrations, the Soviet Union was provided with the information they needed to construct an atomic bomb. After a lengthy FBI investigation, Julius, Ethel, and David were convicted of espionage in 1951. David was sentenced to 15 years in prison, while the Rosenbergs were executed in 1953.

Answers on page 180.

The Watergate Saga

AERIAL	EVENTUAL	OFFICE
AUTHORITIES	EXHAUSTIVE	POLITICAL
BUILDING	FILES	RESIGNATION
BURGLARY	FORMER	SAGA
CENTER	FOUND	SERIES
COMPLEX	GATE	SUSPICIOUS
CORRUPTION	HISTORY	TAPED
CRIME	INCIDENT	TELETYPE
DEMOCRATIC	INGRAINED	UNRAVELING
EARLY	INVALUABLE	VIEW
END	MORNING	

When a night guard at the Watergate hotel and office complex in Washington, D.C. was making his rounds on June 17, 1972, he noticed an exit door that had been suspiciously propped open. Police soon discovered that a break-in had occurred at the Democratic National Committee Headquarters, and when the FBI investigated, they learned that the intruders were connected to the campaign staff of President Richard Nixon.

T	I	B	Y	E	B	B	H	I	S	T	O	R	Y	C	P	U
E	N	T	F	M	V	U	X	E	V	E	N	T	U	A	L	P
Q	C	Y	A	A	N	I	R	M	O	R	N	I	N	G	V	U
S	I	I	L	P	E	O	T	G	T	I	S	E	R	I	E	S
R	D	E	F	R	E	C	I	S	L	F	O	R	M	E	R	C
E	E	P	E	F	A	D	R	T	U	A	A	G	A	S	G	I
T	N	Y	B	T	O	E	U	I	A	A	R	E	Y	N	Y	T
N	T	T	U	L	A	N	U	E	M	N	H	Y	V	W	G	A
E	V	E	I	M	G	G	R	Q	O	E	G	X	D	N	E	R
C	D	L	L	I	X	I	Q	F	U	Q	Q	I	E	U	C	C
X	N	E	D	N	A	S	U	O	I	C	I	P	S	U	S	O
Y	U	T	I	L	A	U	T	H	O	R	I	T	I	E	S	M
B	O	F	N	H	S	E	L	I	F	N	S	J	J	H	R	E
F	F	N	G	V	C	O	R	R	U	P	T	I	O	N	I	D
X	E	L	P	M	O	C	Z	L	A	C	I	T	I	L	O	P
F	D	E	N	I	A	R	G	N	I	L	E	V	A	R	N	U
S	O	V	I	E	W	I	N	V	A	L	U	A	B	L	E	A

Further inquiries brought to light Nixon's attempts to cover up his connection to the burglary, and in 1974, after articles of impeachment were drawn up against him, he resigned from the presidency.

Answers on page 180.

Weather Underground Bombings

ACTIVE	FIELD	PROMOTE
CAPTURED	FLOORS	PROTEST
CRACKS	GROUP	PURSUED
CREDIT	HEADQUARTERS	RESILIENT
CRIME	HOURS	RESPONSIBILITY
DAMAGE	IDENTITIES	ROCKED
DETONATORS	INDUCTION	SHADOWY
DEVICES	JOINT	TACTICS
DISRUPT	MEMBERS	TURBULENT
DYNAMITE	NAME	WEATHER
EXPLODED	OFFSHOOT	

Between 1975 and 1976, more than two dozen bombings occurred across the country, including at the U.S. Capitol, the Pentagon, the California Attorney General's Office, and a New York City police station. The bombers—a domestic terrorist group that called themselves the Weather Underground and embraced violent, communist ideologies—took credit for their work immediately.

N	O	I	T	C	U	D	N	I	P	R	O	T	E	S	T	O
Z	H	F	V	D	I	S	R	U	P	T	D	D	T	R	O	R
S	E	E	T	O	M	O	R	P	J	L	G	E	A	E	D	O
P	A	T	N	E	I	L	I	S	E	R	T	R	C	H	Y	C
U	D	P	K	B	S	C	Q	I	Y	U	O	U	T	T	N	K
R	Q	M	B	T	I	K	F	I	A	S	O	T	I	A	A	E
S	U	E	S	N	Z	N	C	X	D	K	H	P	C	E	M	D
U	A	M	S	E	D	A	M	A	G	E	S	A	S	W	I	D
E	R	B	E	L	I	R	E	I	R	R	F	C	D	C	T	S
D	T	E	C	U	Z	T	X	X	O	C	F	L	R	O	E	W
S	E	R	I	B	P	X	I	T	P	E	O	I	S	L	W	E
R	R	S	V	R	W	H	A	T	M	L	M	D	N	A	V	Y
O	S	E	E	U	W	N	O	A	N	E	O	J	O	I	N	T
O	E	X	D	T	O	J	N	U	J	E	O	D	T	V	F	S
L	S	P	V	T	T	I	D	E	R	C	D	C	E	Y	Y	S
F	G	V	E	P	U	O	R	G	Q	S	A	I	S	D	G	D
P	B	D	R	E	S	P	O	N	S	I	B	I	L	I	T	Y

The FBI partnered with the New York City Police to create an anti-terrorism task force, and by the mid-80s, many members of the group had been arrested and the rest had disbanded. Today, the FBI still uses joint terrorism task forces to combat threats to our safety.

Answers on page 180.

The Sixteenth Street Baptist Church

ACTIVITIES	DAMAGE	PHYSICAL
ADMISSIBLE	EVIDENCE	POLYGRAPH
AGENT	GENERAL	PRISON
BLOCK	HEINOUS	SEPTEMBER
BOMBING	INTERNAL	STAFF
BUREAU	JUSTICE	STIFLE
CASE	LAUNCHED	TARGET
CHARGES	MEMO	VIOLENT
CONVICT	MICROPHONE	WIRETAPS
COURT	MILITARY	WITNESSES
CRATER	OFFENSE	

On the morning of September 15, 1963, a bomb exploded in the Sixteenth Street Baptist Church in Birmingham, Alabama, killing four young girls and injuring 20 others. The well-known civil rights meeting location had been the target of many previous bomb threats, and an FBI investigation put four KKK members—Robert E.

E	N	O	H	P	O	R	C	I	M	R	E	T	A	R	C	W
V	B	U	R	E	A	U	S	T	I	F	L	E	S	L	Y	S
I	Z	J	T	P	R	B	C	Z	S	E	M	U	D	A	R	T
D	L	U	I	F	O	I	W	D	K	C	O	L	B	U	A	A
E	W	S	U	M	V	F	L	B	C	N	W	X	T	N	T	F
N	I	T	B	N	K	R	K	I	I	H	L	O	K	C	I	F
C	T	I	O	A	Q	Y	E	E	W	T	A	B	Y	H	L	E
E	N	C	P	E	C	T	H	B	S	I	N	R	F	E	I	T
G	E	E	H	L	H	T	N	S	M	N	R	E	G	D	M	R
L	S	K	P	B	M	P	I	E	A	E	E	E	L	E	X	U
G	S	W	A	I	R	H	G	V	G	B	T	F	T	O	S	O
F	E	I	R	S	C	Y	G	E	I	A	N	P	F	A	I	C
M	S	K	G	S	A	S	G	Z	N	T	I	O	E	O	P	V
Q	E	V	Y	I	S	I	U	X	M	E	I	Q	S	S	S	S
Q	Y	M	L	M	E	C	W	S	H	R	R	E	K	I	S	P
J	H	T	O	D	T	A	R	G	E	T	X	A	S	J	R	K
U	D	W	P	A	P	L	D	A	M	A	G	E	L	X	U	P

Chambliss, Bobby Frank Cherry, Herman Frank Cash, and Thomas E. Blanton, Jr.—at the top of the suspects list. But frightened witnesses and a lack of evidence prevented immediate charges. Fortunately, Chambliss was sentenced to life in prison in 1977. Cash died in 1994, but Cherry and Blanton were finally sentenced to life in 2000.

Answers on page 181.

The Barker and Karpis Gang

AGENTS	GANG	PERSPIRATION
BUILDING	GRENADES	PLAN
BULLET	HITCH	PRESIDENT
COMPANY	KIDNAPPED	RANSOM
COTTAGE	LATENT	SODIUM
CRIME	LOOT	TECHNOLOGY
CULPRITS	MINNESOTA	VOLLEYS
EXTRACT	MONEY	WARM
FIGURES	NIGHT	WHITE
FINGERPRINTS	NITRATE	WINDOW
FIREARMS	OFFICE	

In the 1930s, two rich Minnesota businessmen were kidnapped and held for ransom. Both men were later released, but the hunt was on for their kidnappers. Using brand-new discoveries in fingerprint technology, the FBI was able to locate the culprits: a group of bank and train robbers led by Alvin Karpis and brothers Fred and Arthur Barker.

C	E	T	I	H	W	Y	Q	S	F	S	X	J	I	J	H	F
S	T	N	E	G	A	G	M	S	Q	Y	Z	P	T	J	G	U
M	N	A	L	P	E	O	I	O	F	E	D	B	H	Y	R	P
A	E	T	V	N	L	L	L	D	I	L	H	U	G	Z	E	K
B	P	O	F	I	S	O	M	I	N	L	I	L	I	B	N	I
W	S	S	I	T	T	N	R	U	G	O	T	L	N	O	A	D
Y	F	E	R	R	I	H	A	M	E	V	C	E	I	C	D	N
L	I	N	E	A	R	C	W	R	R	D	H	T	O	F	E	A
T	G	N	A	T	P	E	A	A	P	Y	A	M	T	M	S	P
C	U	I	R	E	L	T	Y	K	R	R	P	I	N	O	X	P
A	R	M	M	N	U	K	O	E	I	A	Y	L	E	S	C	E
R	E	G	S	S	C	F	W	P	N	R	D	O	T	N	R	D
T	S	D	G	E	F	O	S	Y	T	O	E	O	A	A	I	S
X	X	A	K	I	D	R	B	N	S	Z	M	T	L	R	M	W
E	N	K	C	N	E	T	N	E	D	I	S	E	R	P	E	N
G	B	E	I	P	T	V	N	N	E	G	A	T	T	O	C	V
K	B	W	G	F	B	U	I	L	D	I	N	G	J	N	N	S

In January 1935, Arthur was arrested in Chicago, and a week later, Fred, along with his mother, "Ma" Barker, were killed in a gunfight with the FBI in Florida. Lastly, Karpis was apprehended in 1936, ending the reign of the Barker/Karpis gang.

Answers on page 181.

Snipers on the Beltway

ANALYST	INJURED	SCOPE
BALLISTIC	INVESTIGATION	SERIAL
BORE	LICENSE	SHOCKING
CHARGE	MAGAZINE	SNIPERS
COMPARTMENT	MATCH	SUSPECT
CONVICTED	MATERIAL	TRIAL
COURT	MORNING	TRIPOD
EXTORTION	OCTOBER	VEHICLE
FINGERPRINT	PASSENGER	VICTIMS
FLEW	ROLE	VIOLATION
HOME	SCENE	

Over 23 days in October of 2002, the Washington, D.C., area was terrorized by a series of random shootings. The attacks, which occurred without warning as residents simply went about their daily lives, left 10 people dead and three more injured. The FBI devoted 400 agents to the case, which was broken wide open when one of the snipers called a hotline and admitted to robbing a liquor store in Alabama.

T C E P S U S P B S E R I A L B I
E N I Z A G A M M A T E R I A L J
I T N E S H G R E G N E S S A P M
J N O V U B B S N A N A L Y S T E
S E I I S F O I D T R U O C N G I
R M T C V C N R H E E V W D R F N
E T A T M R D V E S R E D A X I V
P R L I O B G E R N Y U H I D N E
I A O M F A N A T E M C J U O G S
N P I S M L I T G C B F P N P E T
S M V A S L K R N I I O I X I R I
H O T C E I C I D L F V T G R P G
G C O M Q S O A G R Q L N C T R A
H P O N Y T H L O T J O E O O I T
E H E U S I S L E N E C S W C N I
F L P Z X C E E L C I H E V K T O
F E X T O R T I O N M H S X F V N

Following a line of evidence led authorities to John Muhammad and Lee Malvo, who were arrested on October 24. Malvo was sentenced to life in prison, and Muhammad received the death penalty.

Answers on page 181.

The Black Tom Railroad Yard Bombing

ACT	ERUPTED	SHRAPNEL
ALLY	EVAPORATED	SKY
BABY	EVEN	SOIL
BLEW	MUNITIONS	SQUAD
BOMB	NEUTRAL	THOUSANDS
CONFLICT	PARK	TONS
CONGRESS	PRESIDENTIAL	VARIETY
CULPRITS	PROVOCATION	VULNERABILITY
DOGGEDLY	RAILROAD	WAR
EMPLOYEES	SABOTEURS	YARD
ENEMY	SECURITY	

The first World War was in full swing in 1916, with the United States choosing to remain neutral at the beginning of the conflict. But that didn't stop German agents from setting off a bomb at the Black Tom railroad yard in Manhattan on July 30. The explosion shattered thousands of windows and killed four people, one of them a baby.

T	H	O	U	S	A	N	D	S	L	A	R	T	U	E	N	B
P	D	A	O	R	L	I	A	R	P	D	E	N	E	M	Y	M
C	R	L	K	S	H	K	I	G	O	X	C	J	W	A	R	O
W	S	E	D	K	R	T	R	G	K	O	A	O	S	G	I	B
V	E	Y	S	S	S	U	G	A	N	Y	T	E	I	R	A	V
U	C	S	J	I	P	E	E	G	P	H	E	Y	T	L	N	C
L	U	H	S	L	D	Y	R	T	M	Y	M	C	B	O	W	U
N	R	R	Y	L	L	E	N	U	O	H	A	G	I	D	Z	L
E	I	A	Y	L	S	E	N	L	U	B	C	T	A	E	C	P
R	T	P	A	S	V	I	P	T	K	K	A	B	I	T	G	R
A	Y	N	I	E	T	M	Y	P	I	C	A	S	Q	A	E	I
B	K	E	S	I	E	L	Y	A	O	A	S	D	X	R	R	T
I	S	L	O	S	O	I	L	V	R	Q	L	D	Y	O	U	S
L	H	N	S	B	N	V	O	D	U	D	Q	B	G	P	P	C
I	S	K	N	L	C	R	W	A	Z	E	A	L	E	A	T	C
T	O	W	O	E	P	M	D	J	V	B	U	W	L	V	E	I
Y	V	T	T	W	C	O	N	F	L	I	C	T	B	E	D	J

With the help of the NYPD's bomb squad, the newly created FBI was eventually able to discover the identity of the culprits. When the war was over, Germany paid the United States reparations to atone for the attack against a neutral country.

Answers on page 181.

Brian P. Regan Espionage

ACCEPT	DOCUMENTS	POSSESSION
ARREST	ENCODED	SELL
BOARD	ENCRYPTED	SENTENCE
BURIED	ESPIONAGE	SIGN
CLASSIFIED	FOREIGN	STASH
COMPACT	INTELLIGENCE	STOLEN
COMPUTER	JURY	TACTICAL
CONTACT	MATERIALS	TROVE
CONVICTED	NETWORK	UNDERGROUND
DIPLOMATIC	OFFICES	VIDEOTAPES
DISKS	PAGES	

On August 23, 2001, FBI agents arrested former Air Force intelligence officer Brian P. Regan as he attempted to board a flight to Switzerland at Dulles International Airport. The father of four had accrued a crippling amount of debt, and planned to sell stolen classified material from the National Reconnaissance Office to China, Iraq, and Libya in exchange for $13 million.

P	S	C	C	H	B	S	L	A	I	R	E	T	A	M	C	E
O	D	I	A	O	P	O	N	N	G	I	E	R	O	F	C	G
S	S	T	E	O	N	S	A	G	R	V	T	D	M	U	O	A
S	T	A	C	C	F	V	J	R	I	I	R	E	G	E	T	N
E	O	M	N	O	I	F	I	Y	D	S	O	I	S	C	N	O
S	L	O	E	N	S	E	I	C	R	N	V	F	E	N	E	I
S	E	L	T	T	F	K	O	C	T	U	E	I	P	E	T	P
I	N	P	N	A	S	D	S	X	E	E	J	S	A	G	W	S
O	M	I	E	C	N	E	T	I	N	S	D	S	T	I	O	E
N	V	D	S	T	P	S	L	C	D	C	A	A	O	L	R	T
E	A	C	C	E	P	T	F	L	A	P	L	L	E	L	K	A
N	L	A	C	I	T	C	A	T	C	P	U	C	D	E	U	R
C	T	Y	C	O	M	P	U	T	E	R	M	E	I	T	U	R
O	X	D	O	C	U	M	E	N	T	S	I	O	V	N	J	E
D	E	N	C	R	Y	P	T	E	D	R	J	N	C	I	K	S
E	U	N	D	E	R	G	R	O	U	N	D	E	S	F	M	T
D	B	H	S	A	T	S	S	B	S	E	G	A	P	F	R	I

Regan had cleverly buried the materials, which included documents, videotapes, and CDs, in state parks in Maryland and Virginia. In exchange for a life sentence, he led authorities to all of the buried classified material.

Answers on page 182.

Weinberger Kidnapping

APPEALS	DROVE	PERSONAL
AVERAGE	EVIDENCE	RANSOM
BABY	FALLOUT	RESIDENTS
BOOTLEGGING	HANDWRITING	SHOWED
CARRIAGE	INFANT	SITE
CENTURY	LEGISLATION	SNATCHED
COMPARISONS	MINUTES	SUBURBAN
CURB	NATIONAL	SWARMED
DEMAND	NEWSPAPERS	TARGETED
DIAPER	PARTICULAR	THREAT
DISPATCHER	PATIO	

When Morris and Betty Weinberger's infant son, Peter, was kidnapped from their front porch on July 4, 1956, it stunned the entire country. The only clue left behind was a handwritten ransom note, demanding $2,000. At the time, the FBI was required to wait for seven days before involving themselves in a kidnapping case, so when local authorities had no leads after a week, the agency

R	A	L	U	C	I	T	R	A	P	G	R	N	I	H	T	F
S	C	M	M	O	S	N	A	R	N	Q	A	D	N	T	U	I
T	A	I	D	P	M	Y	E	I	P	B	N	E	F	H	O	D
N	R	N	T	Y	B	P	G	E	R	A	N	M	A	R	L	U
E	R	U	I	A	A	G	R	U	T	C	B	A	N	E	L	D
D	I	T	B	I	E	S	B	I	M	O	F	N	T	A	A	I
I	A	E	D	L	O	U	O	U	O	M	G	D	F	T	F	S
S	G	S	T	N	S	N	E	W	S	P	A	P	E	R	S	P
E	E	O	A	D	A	Z	A	T	P	A	T	I	O	E	Y	A
R	O	L	C	L	Y	W	C	T	G	R	O	K	E	S	R	T
B	I	I	N	O	I	T	A	L	S	I	G	E	L	L	U	C
S	N	A	T	C	H	E	D	Z	N	S	B	E	S	A	T	H
Y	A	V	E	R	A	G	E	C	Z	O	R	V	I	E	N	E
Y	E	C	N	E	D	I	V	E	P	N	U	O	T	P	E	R
F	S	W	A	R	M	E	D	Y	E	S	C	R	E	P	C	R
H	A	N	D	W	R	I	T	I	N	G	I	D	R	A	U	Y
H	W	R	S	H	O	W	E	D	T	A	R	G	E	T	E	D

stepped in and analyzed the note. They were able to match the handwriting to a truck driver named Angelo LaMarca. Sadly, Peter's body was found lying in brush near the highway, and LaMarca was later executed for murder. Today, the FBI is only required to wait 24 hours before investigating a kidnapping.

Answers on page 182.

Child Kidnappers Go to Jail

ABDUCTORS	HANDCUFFED	PROCEED
ADMITTED	HIDEOUT	PROMINENT
BLANKET	HOLE	RANSOM
CHAUFFEUR	HOME	REGISTER
CLOTH	HOTEL	RESISTANCE
COMPLYING	INSANE	SENTENCED
CURRENCY	LETTER	SERIAL
DIRT	MEET	SHORTCUT
DISAPPEARED	MISSING	SIGNATURE
ENVELOPE	NEGOTIATE	YARDS
FACTS	ORDERS	

On May 24, 1935, nine-year-old George Weyerhaeuser disappeared on the walk home from his Tacoma, Washington, school. His family notified the police, and later that evening received a ransom note demanding $200,000 and providing other instructions. Thankfully, George was released unharmed on June 1, after the ransom was paid.

L	E	T	O	H	O	U	M	I	S	S	I	N	G	V	C	R
C	Q	M	D	Q	T	U	O	E	D	I	H	G	Q	A	H	I
S	L	A	O	E	D	E	F	F	U	C	D	N	A	H	A	L
S	I	O	N	Z	R	D	E	T	T	I	M	D	A	K	U	E
E	D	G	T	E	O	A	E	Z	B	W	Y	P	C	F	F	T
N	T	C	N	H	N	K	E	G	S	E	R	I	A	L	F	T
T	U	R	U	A	N	V	T	P	E	P	Z	I	M	D	E	E
E	C	Y	E	A	T	K	E	N	P	R	K	O	J	E	U	R
N	T	X	L	G	D	U	Z	L	E	A	S	Y	Q	E	R	G
C	R	B	N	I	I	N	R	S	O	N	S	P	C	C	T	N
E	O	P	R	Y	S	S	I	E	A	P	I	I	J	O	E	I
D	H	T	A	T	S	S	T	R	L	F	E	M	D	R	E	Y
O	S	R	C	R	T	P	Y	E	T	U	K	J	O	P	M	L
C	D	A	E	A	L	C	U	R	R	E	N	C	Y	R	S	P
S	F	D	N	A	B	D	U	C	T	O	R	S	J	M	P	M
E	R	C	H	O	L	E	E	T	A	I	T	O	G	E	N	O
O	E	H	O	M	E	E	N	A	S	N	I	I	M	H	W	C

The FBI had carefully recorded the serial numbers on the ransom money and began tracking its location. The kidnappers, Harmon and Margaret Waley and William Dainard, were all located and sentenced to a total of 135 years in prison. Young George fared much better: he went on to become the chairman of the board of Weyerhaeuser Company.

 Answers on page 182.

The Brink's Building Robbery

ARMED	ENTRANCE	MOUTH
BAGS	EVENING	NEWS
BOSTON	FRUITFUL	OFFICIAL
BUZZER	GAG	OPERATION
CAP	GLASSES	POLICE
CASH	GLOVES	PURSUE
CHECKS	GROUP	QUICKLY
CITIZEN	GUNPOINT	ROBBERS
CONFRONTED	LOOT	SECURITIES
CUSTOMERS	MEMBERS	TAPE
EMERGED	MONEY	

On January 17, 1950, a gang of criminals entered the Brink's building in Boston, Massachusetts, and made off with more than $2.7 million in cash, checks, and money orders. The robbers wore masks to conceal their identities and left behind very few clues. Within hours, local authorities and the FBI began an investigation, concentrating on known criminals in the Boston area.

F	Z	U	K	G	R	G	N	I	N	E	V	E	G	A	G	E
R	O	B	B	E	R	S	R	C	E	L	B	A	N	S	P	C
I	O	B	Z	A	N	H	R	J	W	M	O	O	E	L	F	I
D	Q	Z	V	P	S	K	C	E	H	C	E	V	S	R	Q	L
S	U	Z	P	N	T	A	P	E	O	C	O	R	U	T	S	O
B	I	M	O	U	T	H	C	Z	I	L	R	I	G	E	O	P
C	C	R	W	F	O	N	F	T	G	J	T	U	C	E	G	N
U	K	V	X	H	A	R	I	B	L	F	I	U	Z	L	D	T
S	L	Q	T	R	S	Z	G	N	U	A	R	M	E	D	K	W
T	Y	L	T	W	E	P	T	L	O	I	I	M	T	A	H	V
O	K	N	E	N	L	A	S	G	T	I	O	C	H	X	T	L
M	E	N	B	O	P	C	A	I	L	N	T	B	I	S	H	B
E	A	X	O	U	V	E	E	U	E	A	Y	A	F	F	A	K
R	D	T	R	G	A	S	M	Y	O	P	S	G	R	Y	F	C
S	G	S	S	R	E	B	M	E	M	V	Y	S	F	E	C	O
Y	U	C	O	N	F	R	O	N	T	E	D	F	E	A	P	M
E	Z	T	N	I	O	P	N	U	G	S	F	M	U	S	B	O

Although they narrowed their search to about a dozen likely suspects, it took six years and thousands of dead-end leads to finally zero in on the culprits. With the help of gang member Joseph James O'Keefe, who confessed to the crime and agreed to testify against his co-conspirators, eight men were finally sentenced for the crime in 1956.

Answers on page 182.

The Charles Ross Kidnapping

ABDUCTION	ELECTROCUTION	NEGOTIATONS
AMOUNT	EVIDENT	PAIR
ASSOCIATE	EXTORTION	PRESIDENT
BANDIT	GREETING	RACETRACK
BANK	HISTORY	RANSOM
CHICAGO	ILLINOIS	TRAP
CLUE	KIDNAPPING	UNRAVEL
DARKNESS	LOCATION	WEALTHY
DEMANDS	MANHUNTS	WISCONSIN
DETECTION	MOTORCYCLE	YOUTHFUL
DRIVING	MURDERS	

On September 25, 1937, the wealthy president of a greeting card company, Charles Ross, was kidnapped by John Henry Seadlund and James Atwood Gray. The abductors mailed four ransom notes demanding $50,000 for Ross's return. Ross's family complied, but Seadlund decided not to share the ransom money with Gray. Their ensuing argument left both Gray and Ross dead.

E	C	S	T	N	U	H	N	A	M	B	K	T	L	E	U	K
T	Z	N	O	I	T	R	O	T	X	E	R	P	U	L	N	A
A	N	W	D	R	I	V	I	N	G	A	R	F	F	E	R	E
I	N	U	I	V	K	I	I	B	P	E	Z	O	H	C	A	P
C	J	E	O	S	D	C	C	R	S	Y	G	T	T	T	V	N
O	D	L	G	M	C	C	A	I	A	A	B	Q	U	R	E	E
S	Q	S	O	O	A	O	D	R	C	N	D	R	O	O	L	G
S	G	S	T	A	T	E	N	I	T	E	S	L	Y	C	Y	N
A	N	E	N	H	N	I	H	S	T	E	K	O	Y	U	H	I
V	I	N	E	T	I	C	A	E	I	N	C	C	M	T	T	T
S	P	K	D	U	L	S	C	T	A	N	R	A	O	I	L	E
D	P	R	I	H	L	T	T	B	O	O	T	T	R	O	A	E
N	A	A	V	F	I	C	P	O	T	N	I	I	R	N	E	R
A	N	D	E	O	N	Y	S	O	R	E	S	O	D	I	W	G
M	D	Y	N	S	O	D	M	V	L	Y	W	N	W	N	A	I
E	I	G	M	K	I	S	R	E	D	R	U	M	Y	M	A	P
D	K	B	N	V	S	V	A	B	D	U	C	T	I	O	N	B

The FBI tracked the serial numbers on the ransom money and closed in on Seadlund at a racetrack in Los Angeles, where he was apprehended. He confessed his crimes to the first director of the FBI, J. Edgar Hoover, and was executed on July 14, 1938.

 Answers on page 183.

Fritz Duquesne, Nazi Spy

AGGRESSION	DETONATION	GUILTY
AHEAD	DIESEL	HATRED
AIRCRAFT	DOCKS	MASSIVE
AIRTIGHT	DOUBLE	NATIVE
CARGOES	DYNAMITE	NAZI
CITIZEN	ENEMY	PERSONA
CODED	EQUIPMENT	PLED
CONCURRENT	FAMILY	RINGLEADER
CONSULATE	FREQUENCIES	SHOT
COOPERATE	FUNDS	TRANSMIT
DEFENSE	GROUP	

Just before the United States was pulled into World War II, a German-American by the name of William Sebold proved invaluable to the country. On a trip to Germany to visit his mother in 1939, Sebold was approached by Nazi agents who asked the naturalized U.S. citizen to spy for their cause.

C	D	O	C	K	S	F	A	M	I	L	Y	E	G	P	U	E
E	S	D	N	U	F	U	C	I	T	I	Z	E	N	L	H	T
V	S	N	N	U	I	A	E	V	I	S	S	A	M	E	E	A
C	E	T	C	Z	T	I	M	S	N	A	R	T	M	D	N	L
R	I	A	A	N	O	I	S	S	E	R	G	G	A	E	E	U
I	C	N	R	L	E	S	E	I	D	A	W	O	D	Q	M	S
F	N	W	G	Y	Q	A	D	A	I	Y	N	N	Y	U	Y	N
E	E	T	O	W	R	A	N	R	N	D	A	I	N	I	G	O
L	U	F	E	W	E	E	T	O	E	R	E	W	A	P	C	C
B	Q	A	S	H	H	I	D	T	S	T	C	Y	M	M	C	E
U	E	R	A	A	G	R	O	A	A	R	T	Q	I	E	O	S
O	R	C	T	H	I	N	T	R	E	L	E	U	T	N	D	N
D	F	R	T	K	A	E	E	W	I	L	P	P	E	T	E	E
N	E	I	C	T	L	P	V	U	E	W	G	U	T	T	D	F
D	I	A	I	R	O	Q	G	P	H	T	Z	N	O	O	N	E
S	B	O	C	O	N	C	U	R	R	E	N	T	I	R	H	D
E	N	S	C	K	Q	Z	E	V	I	T	A	N	D	R	G	S

Sebold agreed, but secretly contacted U.S. authorities and instead became an informant for the FBI. Sebold identified dozens of Nazi spies in New York, including Fritz Duquesne, the ringleader of a Nazi spy organization. Thanks to Sebold, by the time the U.S. entered the war, every member of Duquesne's spy ring had been arrested.

Answers on page 183.

Soviet Espionage in the 1970s

AGAIN	DROVE	OFFICIALS
ARRESTS	EAST	OPERATIONS
BETWEEN	EXPELLED	PICKED
BOOTHS	FELT	POSSIBLE
BUSY	GAME	SITE
CANISTERS	KEY	SOVIET
CASH	LETTER	STATION
CLASSIFIED	MAGNETIC	STILTED
COVERT	MATERIAL	TRIAL
DISSIDENT	MESSAGES	TURNPIKE
DROP	MOUSE	

In 1977, the FBI suspected that the Soviets were using their offices at the U.N. as a front for espionage. To prove their suspicions, they launched Operation Lemon Aid, in which they recruited Navy lieutenant commander Art Lindberg to pose as a man willing to betray his country.

P	X	T	L	E	F	X	S	N	O	I	T	A	R	E	P	O
U	I	L	T	O	F	F	I	C	I	A	L	S	P	F	L	P
S	E	G	A	S	S	E	M	D	S	T	S	E	R	R	A	R
R	K	C	P	M	T	S	E	D	I	S	S	I	D	E	N	T
Q	I	I	U	S	O	B	O	O	T	H	S	U	Z	Z	Q	X
E	P	T	A	J	O	Z	D	E	I	F	I	S	S	A	L	C
T	N	E	P	I	C	K	E	D	B	D	E	T	L	I	T	S
I	R	N	Z	Q	L	T	C	E	E	S	D	W	D	A	P	S
S	U	G	F	H	R	O	T	L	R	H	I	R	R	X	O	O
H	T	A	E	I	V	W	B	E	D	S	R	G	O	E	X	V
Z	B	M	A	E	E	I	T	N	E	A	E	I	P	V	L	I
Q	L	L	R	E	S	S	O	S	L	C	N	C	I	M	E	E
B	E	T	N	S	I	I	D	E	L	F	V	I	O	G	C	T
U	T	I	O	N	T	X	L	N	E	D	V	U	A	V	Y	C
S	T	P	A	A	X	T	D	H	P	V	S	M	N	G	D	U
Y	E	C	T	U	M	K	E	Y	X	E	E	K	C	Z	A	A
L	R	S	B	J	G	M	A	T	E	R	I	A	L	I	O	O

Lindberg passed along declassified information to the Soviets, convincing them he was selling "secrets" of the U.S. Navy. Meanwhile, the FBI kept tabs on their communication, and soon had enough evidence to arrest two KGB officers, Valdik Enger and Rudolf Chernyayev. The pair became the first Soviet officials tried for espionage in the U.S.

 Answers on page 183.

Telemarketing Fraud

BOILER	INDIVIDUALS	PSYCHOLOGICAL
CONVERSATIONS	INFORMANT	RETIREMENT
CONVICTIONS	JAIL	ROLE
DENT	LOAN	ROOM
DISCOURAGED	MAJOR	STORIES
EARLIER	MESSAGE	TELEMARKETING
EFFECTIVE	NATION	TWIST
FRAUD	OHIO	VICTIM
HEYDAY	OPERATION	VOLUNTEER
HUCKSTER	PARTNERS	WAVE
INDEXED	PHONE	

In the 1990s, telemarketing scammers were running rampant, swindling victims out of an estimated $40 billion total. Using tactics such as collecting for nonexistent charities, these con artists often targeted elderly people on fixed incomes, making their fraud even more despicable.

C	A	Y	H	L	Q	L	H	S	R	E	N	T	R	A	P	Y
V	T	Z	U	R	J	A	T	X	C	R	V	M	U	M	W	S
I	W	S	C	O	U	C	E	B	O	A	O	A	P	E	W	L
C	I	T	K	J	D	I	V	D	N	I	T	O	W	S	K	I
T	S	O	S	A	E	G	I	U	V	N	N	R	M	S	X	A
I	T	R	T	M	G	O	T	A	E	D	A	E	O	A	R	J
M	H	I	E	X	A	L	C	R	R	I	M	I	P	G	E	O
F	B	E	R	E	R	O	E	F	S	V	R	L	E	E	L	R
R	D	S	L	T	U	H	F	N	A	I	O	R	R	D	I	E
P	V	O	N	M	O	C	F	O	T	D	F	A	A	E	O	T
H	R	E	W	L	C	Y	E	I	I	U	N	E	T	X	B	I
O	D	X	O	S	S	S	H	T	O	A	I	R	I	E	R	R
N	O	A	T	D	I	P	Q	A	N	L	Y	H	O	D	N	E
E	N	H	E	Y	D	A	Y	N	S	S	E	Y	N	N	D	M
S	N	O	I	T	C	I	V	N	O	C	K	P	W	I	U	E
T	M	V	O	H	I	O	R	E	E	T	N	U	L	O	V	N
T	E	L	E	M	A	R	K	E	T	I	N	G	H	S	B	T

But the FBI developed a plan to crack down on these cons, using not only FBI agents, but volunteers recruited by the American Association of Retired Persons (AARP). The volunteers recorded their conversations with telemarketers, leading to the arrest of 1,200 fraudsters. Operation Senior Sentinel, as it was named, marked the end of an era of telemarketing scams.

Answers on page 183.

A WWII Double Agent

ALLIED	FINGERED	PROGRESS
BACK	GOOD	RADIO
BOSSES	HIGHLY	SECLUDED
BROADCASTS	IDENTITIES	STRING
BUREAU	INTELLIGENCE	TELEGRAPH
CAME	INVASION	TENSION
CLATTER	KEY	TRANSMISSION
CLEARED	MADE	TURN
COMPLY	MESSAGE	VALUE
CONVINCE	OPERATIONS	WIDER
DOUBLE	PHASES	

In the early 1940s, the FBI managed to identify many German spies living in America and successfully turned them to the Allied side, giving the U.S. an advantage through "double agents." One such agent was known by the code name ND-98. Sending messages from a secluded Long

A	B	A	C	K	K	C	W	D	E	R	E	G	N	I	F	Y
U	A	E	R	U	B	X	N	S	V	C	S	T	W	I	K	I
O	R	J	R	M	N	R	G	A	E	N	A	W	N	D	A	H
I	H	B	A	G	U	O	L	D	O	S	T	M	P	E	W	X
D	H	I	R	T	Z	U	I	I	C	R	A	R	E	N	C	U
A	P	B	W	O	E	J	T	S	A	L	O	H	B	T	O	S
R	A	S	X	I	A	A	D	N	A	G	A	N	P	I	M	E
E	R	E	Q	M	R	D	S	O	R	V	M	T	G	T	P	C
G	G	S	A	E	A	M	C	E	U	R	N	O	T	I	L	L
A	E	S	P	L	I	D	S	A	C	B	O	I	C	E	Y	U
S	L	O	X	S	L	S	E	L	S	D	L	V	Y	S	R	D
S	E	B	S	Z	X	I	E	S	C	T	M	E	X	R	X	E
E	T	I	U	S	T	A	E	N	O	I	S	N	E	T	I	D
M	O	C	Y	T	R	H	O	D	W	H	I	G	H	L	Y	D
N	R	E	W	E	I	N	T	E	L	L	I	G	E	N	C	E
A	K	Z	D	J	N	I	H	S	T	R	I	N	G	Q	G	S
C	O	N	V	I	N	C	E	S	T	D	D	R	E	D	I	W

Island home, ND-98 provided the Abwehr, the Nazi intelligence service, with information. But much of that information was deliberately false, in order to misdirect the Nazis and benefit the Allies. Thanks to the efforts of ND-98 and other double agents, the Allies welcomed many victories on the battlefield against the Nazis.

 Answers on page 184.

The FBI and the U.S. Criminal Code

ABOARD	DRUG	PIRACY
ACTIONS	EYED	RENDEZVOUS
AIRLINER	HIJACKERS	ROYAL
AMERICANS	HOSTAGES	SENTENCED
AUTHORITY	IMPLICATED	STEAMED
BECKONED	INTERNATIONAL	SUSPECTED
BRIGHT	JORDAN	TARMAC
CAREER	LUCRATIVE	TERRORISM
CASE	MOTORBOAT	YACHT
CONSPIRACY	NAVY	YEAR
DECK	PASSAGE	

In 1985, terrorists hijacked a Royal Jordanian airliner, forcing terrified passengers, including two Americans, on a journey from Cyprus to Sicily to Beirut. There, the terrorists freed the hostages, but then blew up the plane before fleeing. The event led to new legislation in the U.S. Criminal Code that allows the FBI to conduct investigations abroad when terrorist acts are committed against Americans.

A	P	K	C	E	D	C	E	V	I	T	A	R	C	U	L	E
S	E	G	A	T	S	O	H	Y	T	I	R	O	H	T	U	A
J	Y	D	E	T	C	E	P	S	U	S	I	C	Q	Q	I	Y
S	E	G	A	S	S	A	P	R	E	K	M	Q	V	R	N	C
S	U	O	V	Z	E	D	N	E	R	L	P	J	E	S	T	A
B	E	C	K	O	N	E	D	K	V	S	L	N	G	T	E	R
K	M	A	R	O	Y	A	L	C	T	Z	I	K	Y	E	R	I
Z	O	C	C	Z	Q	H	I	A	E	L	C	R	V	A	N	P
P	T	B	A	T	S	O	G	J	R	P	A	J	A	M	A	S
I	O	R	P	R	I	N	H	I	R	A	T	T	N	E	T	N
R	R	I	D	R	E	O	A	H	O	B	E	Y	E	D	I	O
A	B	G	N	K	T	E	N	C	R	O	D	V	Y	N	O	C
C	O	H	G	H	U	D	R	S	I	A	U	W	E	A	N	F
Y	A	T	C	Q	R	O	E	K	S	R	I	Y	A	D	A	M
V	T	A	A	U	E	S	J	G	M	D	E	B	R	R	L	E
Z	Y	P	G	T	A	R	M	A	C	M	F	M	S	O	L	F
Z	A	D	E	C	N	E	T	N	E	S	U	Q	A	J	T	W

The agency made use of the new law in 1987 during Operation Goldenrod, when agents lured Fawaz Younis, one of the terrorists, onto a yacht in the Mediterranean with the promise of a drug deal. Instead, he was arrested and sentenced to 30 years in prison.

 Answers on page 184.

Kidnapping Frank Sinatra's Son

BLINDFOLDED	INFAMOUS	RANSOM
BOLD	KIDNAPPERS	RICH
CAPTURED	MORNING	ROADBLOCKS
CAREER	MOTHER	SINGER
CITY	MUSIC	SNATCH
CONSPIRATOR	NERVOUS	STRIKE
CONTACT	NOOSE	SUBURB
DEMANDED	PACKAGE	TARGET
DROP	PAIR	TRUNK
HEFTY	PLAN	VICTIM
HIDEOUT	PROGRESS	

There may have been no more famous singer in America in the 1950s and 60s than "Old Blue Eyes," Frank Sinatra. And in 1963, three men—Barry Keenan, Joe Amsler, and John Irwin—attempted to capitalize on that popularity by kidnapping the wealthy singer's son, Frank Sinatra Jr., after the younger singer had finished a show in Lake Tahoe.

S	V	G	C	A	P	T	U	R	E	D	D	L	E	B	E	J
R	D	Q	B	C	J	M	O	R	N	I	N	G	U	P	G	Q
E	U	E	L	L	T	H	C	T	A	N	S	U	O	C	A	C
P	C	Z	M	U	I	H	N	A	L	P	X	R	I	P	K	I
P	K	M	G	A	C	N	S	E	K	F	D	T	R	R	C	S
A	N	J	M	I	N	U	D	P	K	C	Y	O	N	E	A	U
N	U	T	R	V	O	D	A	F	O	I	G	L	R	E	P	M
D	R	G	U	V	S	I	E	N	O	R	R	O	H	R	C	J
I	T	I	R	O	R	K	T	D	E	L	T	T	G	A	S	I
K	L	E	B	L	E	A	C	S	W	A	D	R	S	C	I	N
C	N	P	R	Z	C	D	S	O	R	O	E	E	M	I	N	F
P	O	V	U	T	T	H	I	I	L	H	E	O	D	I	G	A
E	G	H	B	F	M	A	P	H	T	B	S	S	L	N	E	M
M	A	E	U	C	F	S	R	O	F	N	D	G	O	G	R	O
P	D	F	S	A	N	Y	M	G	A	N	Q	A	B	O	P	U
K	W	T	A	O	Y	O	Q	R	E	T	O	S	O	U	N	S
F	A	Y	C	W	T	P	V	I	C	T	I	M	A	R	N	N

The trio demanded a $240,000 ransom, which Sinatra Sr. gave to the FBI so the agency could track it. Irwin, however, had a change of heart and freed Sinatra Jr., then confessed to the crime. Keenan and Amsler were soon arrested, the ransom money was recovered, and all were convicted.

 Answers on page 184.

Machine Gun Kelly

ATTEMPT	GARAGE	PISTOL
BERTH	GAS	PORCH
BRIDGE	HOME	PUBLIC
CONSEQUENCE	HOTEL	RESIDENCE
COUPLES	INCIDENT	TELEPHONE
DAYS	INTERFERE	TRACK
DENOMINATION	LICENSE	VALUE
DUMMY	MACHINE	WARNING
ELAPSED	NATURE	WEALTHY
ERROR	OUTSKIRTS	WRITER
FRIENDS	PACKAGE	

Born in 1897, George R. Kelly's nickname "Machine Gun" was bestowed by his wife, Kathryn Thorne, who encouraged his life of crime. After a few years as a bootlegger and bank robber, Kelly abducted a wealthy Oklahoma City man named Charles Urschel in 1933. Kelly and his associates held Urschel on property near Paradise, Texas, that was owned by his wife's family.

Q	F	B	P	I	S	T	O	L	C	I	L	B	U	P	S	N
S	W	S	S	C	P	B	I	S	M	A	C	H	I	N	E	A
C	E	E	P	M	H	C	D	A	Y	S	J	U	P	O	S	T
N	A	K	E	O	E	T	R	A	C	K	S	A	G	Y	D	U
V	L	T	M	N	I	N	C	I	D	E	N	T	B	F	T	R
E	T	E	S	E	R	E	F	R	E	T	N	I	D	S	X	E
A	H	E	X	N	E	C	N	E	U	Q	E	S	N	O	C	R
E	Y	V	E	O	N	O	I	T	A	N	I	M	O	N	E	D
C	N	A	Q	H	I	P	E	E	G	A	K	C	A	P	I	C
N	E	L	A	P	S	E	D	G	T	F	S	T	D	P	O	H
E	Y	U	A	E	H	Q	R	Q	A	A	R	U	D	U	A	C
D	G	E	W	L	O	H	E	E	Z	R	M	I	P	X	M	R
I	B	D	E	E	T	T	T	R	N	M	A	L	E	Z	V	O
S	I	M	I	T	E	R	I	R	Y	P	E	G	W	N	I	P
E	E	N	F	R	L	E	R	O	D	S	Q	X	X	K	D	W
R	D	D	U	V	B	B	W	R	G	N	I	N	R	A	W	S
G	D	U	N	S	T	R	I	K	S	T	U	O	P	M	K	X

After a ransom of $200,000 was paid, Urschel was released; but unluckily for Kelly and his accomplices, Urschel was able to provide the FBI with a detailed description of the area he was held. Agents arrested 21 people in connection with the case, and Kelly and his wife were given life sentences.

Answers on page 184.

Gerhard Arthur Puff

AGE	DISORDERLY	MURDER
ASSOCIATE	EXPIRATION	NARROW
ATTEMPT	FIRE	PAIR
ATTORNEY	GUILTY	PENITENTIARY
BANDIT	HAND	POSITION
BANK	HERDED	RADIO
BOND	HOSPITAL	REFORMATORY
COVERALLS	IRREVOCABLE	STAIRWAY
CRIME	KILLER	SURRENDER
DASH	LIFE	WAREHOUSE
DEAD	LOBBY	

Gerhard Arthur Puff was a career criminal. The German native, who became a U.S. citizen in 1934, spent much of his young adulthood in and out of prison. After he met fellow criminal George Arthur Heroux in 1951, the pair cooked up a plan to rob a Kansas bank. They made off with $62,000, but the FBI soon identified the culprits.

L	G	Y	U	D	E	A	D	S	U	R	R	E	N	D	E	R
P	E	N	I	T	E	N	T	I	A	R	Y	R	G	F	E	Y
T	X	E	F	E	T	A	I	C	O	S	S	A	Q	A	R	Y
X	O	I	L	O	B	B	Y	D	E	D	R	E	H	O	L	V
P	R	A	T	T	O	R	N	E	Y	N	B	P	T	R	S	X
E	Q	W	J	H	O	S	P	I	T	A	L	A	E	F	L	E
P	B	I	N	D	K	N	I	N	T	S	M	D	N	L	L	L
D	X	R	A	Q	A	D	O	T	C	R	R	Y	L	K	A	B
N	A	S	D	R	N	I	E	B	O	O	Z	A	R	D	R	A
A	H	F	R	O	T	M	W	F	S	D	B	W	E	V	E	C
H	L	O	B	I	P	G	E	I	N	W	A	R	D	H	V	O
T	W	O	S	T	Y	R	D	C	X	N	N	I	R	L	O	V
C	N	O	I	T	A	R	I	P	X	E	D	A	U	U	C	E
B	P	H	L	I	V	E	M	I	R	C	I	T	M	L	J	R
G	R	I	R	E	L	L	I	K	L	E	T	S	I	P	G	R
U	U	F	O	O	O	I	D	A	R	T	Q	F	I	D	B	I
G	P	A	I	R	T	E	S	U	O	H	E	R	A	W	Q	G

Heroux was arrested in Miami in July 1952. Puff, located in a hotel in New York City, was apprehended after a gun fight that killed FBI agent Joseph John Brock. Now guilty of murder, Puff was sentenced to death and executed in 1954.

Answers on page 185.

TWA Flight 847

ACCOMPLICE	DIVER	MURDER
AIRPORT	DRAGGED	PASSENGERS
ASSAULT	FLIGHT	PISTOLS
BEATING	GRENADES	PROSECUTE
BLANK	HEAD	REFERENCE
CHEEK	HIJACKING	SENTENCED
CITIZEN	HOSTAGE	STOP
COLLABORATORS	INDICTED	TARMAC
CONVICTIONS	INFORMATION	TERRORISTS
CUSTODY	LIVING	THROWN
DARK	MOLE	

On June 14, 1985, terrorists took control of TWA Flight 847. Over the next 17 days, the 153 people aboard endured threats and violence from the hijackers, who included Lebanese citizen Mohammed Ali Hamadei. Pilot John Testrake was ordered to fly the plane between Beirut and Algiers several times, as the terrorists demanded the release of Lebanese prisoners held in Israel.

Q	G	I	C	M	A	N	E	Z	I	T	I	C	O	L	M	C
S	N	K	N	H	E	K	T	C	B	S	S	E	D	S	T	S
T	Q	R	E	F	N	G	A	L	L	K	T	W	N	E	T	B
O	C	A	R	A	O	M	A	O	U	U	E	O	B	A	H	P
P	O	D	L	E	R	R	T	T	C	A	I	E	E	U	R	O
E	L	B	A	A	F	S	M	E	S	T	S	D	H	A	O	S
E	L	D	T	I	I	E	S	A	C	O	E	S	V	C	W	E
C	A	O	E	P	R	O	R	I	T	T	H	T	A	C	N	N
I	B	F	M	G	R	P	V	E	C	I	E	R	U	Y	H	T
L	O	B	L	P	G	N	O	I	N	R	O	S	D	S	I	E
P	R	H	V	I	O	A	D	R	R	C	T	N	I	E	J	N
M	A	R	E	C	G	N	R	O	T	O	E	P	V	D	A	C
O	T	E	K	A	I	H	R	D	D	I	J	S	E	A	C	E
C	O	D	P	B	D	I	T	Y	V	L	O	G	R	N	K	D
C	R	R	P	A	S	S	E	N	G	E	R	S	A	E	I	F
A	S	U	M	T	B	L	G	N	I	T	A	E	B	R	N	L
K	F	M	S	B	U	G	G	N	I	V	I	L	T	G	G	T

Most terrifying of all, 23-year-old passenger Robert Stethem was shot and killed. Hamadei remained at large until January 1987, when he was arrested in Germany. Although he was sentenced to life in prison, he was released in 2005.

Answers on page 185.

The Unabomber

ANALYSIS	FORENSIC	PRIMITIVE
ASPIRES	GENDER	RECLUSE
BASIS	GENIUS	REIGN
BOMBER	GLEANED	SCRAP
BUILDS	HANDWRITTEN	SOPHISTICATED
CATCH	INVESTIGATORS	THEORIES
COMBED	LIVE	TWISTED
COMPONENTS	MAILING	UNTRACEABLE
DELIVERS	MANIFESTO	WISDOM
ESSAY	MOTIVES	WORLD
FALSE	PERFECT	

In 1966, the FBI learned that several Americans were plotting to blow up a railroad bridge in the Republic of Zambia. The question was, why would Americans want to attack a peaceful foreign nation? The answer was discovered after interviewing the culprits, all of whom worked in the copper industry.

R	S	U	S	T	N	E	N	O	P	M	O	C	E	D	Q	V
E	U	N	U	P	L	U	D	J	F	I	M	F	E	E	M	F
I	I	S	A	I	E	E	E	O	I	A	V	T	S	T	O	T
G	N	N	V	A	T	R	R	I	N	J	A	S	E	D	T	W
N	E	E	V	S	S	E	F	I	N	C	A	S	L	E	I	I
S	G	T	I	E	N	P	F	E	I	Y	A	R	B	N	V	S
H	N	W	O	S	S	E	I	T	C	S	M	E	A	A	E	D
S	T	E	I	J	S	T	S	R	X	T	N	V	E	E	S	O
G	E	C	T	T	D	I	I	E	E	Z	T	I	C	L	K	M
N	C	I	O	T	H	D	A	G	S	S	Q	L	A	G	V	W
I	S	F	R	P	I	A	R	N	A	L	Z	E	R	S	G	O
L	O	C	O	O	C	R	C	E	A	T	A	D	T	D	E	R
I	J	S	R	X	E	O	W	A	B	L	O	F	N	L	N	L
A	S	O	N	A	C	H	M	D	T	M	Y	R	U	I	D	D
M	K	F	Q	P	P	S	T	B	N	C	O	S	S	U	E	O
T	P	R	I	M	I	T	I	V	E	A	H	B	I	B	R	A
J	L	J	R	E	C	L	U	S	E	D	H	S	I	S	A	B

As one of the leading producers of copper in the world, Zambia relied on railroads to ship the metal. By blowing up the railroad, the country's copper supply would be disrupted, leading to financial gains in other parts of the world. Fortunately, the plan was thwarted, and the saboteurs were arrested, fined, and jailed.

Answers on page 185.

Terrorist Attack in Yemen

ADDITIONAL	EXTENSIVE	QUICKLY
AGENTS	GUIDANCE	REFUELING
ALONGSIDE	HOLE	SAILORS
ASSISTED	IMPACT	SMALL
BOAT	INJURING	SUICIDE
BOMBING	KILLING	TECHNICIANS
CRIME	MEMBERS	TERRORISTS
DESTROYER	NETWORK	TRAVELED
EVIDENCE	PLANNED	VICTIMS
EXAMINE	PORT	WATER
EXPLODED	PROTOCOLS	

On October 12, 2000, the U.S. Navy destroyer USS Cole was refueling in the Yemeni port of Aden when a small boat pulled up alongside it and exploded. Suicide terrorists had detonated a bomb, ripping a hole in the destroyer and killing 17 American sailors.

S	S	R	E	B	M	E	M	R	E	Y	O	R	T	S	E	D
A	G	E	I	R	W	D	E	L	X	D	E	N	N	A	L	P
I	N	S	S	E	I	E	O	C	E	K	G	W	Z	W	L	W
L	I	T	T	F	T	H	X	M	N	N	L	E	H	A	K	K
O	R	N	S	U	O	E	I	P	I	E	N	L	N	C	A	X
R	U	E	I	E	O	R	C	B	L	E	D	O	A	L	J	V
S	J	G	R	L	C	W	M	H	T	O	I	I	O	M	I	G
A	N	A	O	I	Q	O	E	W	N	T	D	N	V	C	S	U
S	I	R	R	N	B	U	O	D	I	I	G	E	T	E	W	I
L	E	D	R	G	G	R	I	D	I	S	C	I	D	A	T	D
O	N	E	E	P	K	V	D	C	I	C	M	I	T	X	A	A
C	I	L	T	G	F	A	P	D	K	S	I	E	A	R	O	N
O	M	E	X	U	I	W	E	H	N	L	R	U	Q	N	B	C
T	A	V	K	G	N	I	L	L	I	K	Y	N	S	V	S	E
O	X	A	Q	P	I	E	X	T	E	N	S	I	V	E	K	I
R	E	R	R	E	T	V	I	V	A	S	S	I	S	T	E	D
P	P	T	T	R	O	P	I	M	P	A	C	T	R	C	U	S

The FBI counterterrorism division, along with Yemeni investigators, immediately began questioning witnesses and suspects. After combing through evidence, including the USS *Cole* itself, which had been transferred to Pascagoula, Mississippi, agents concluded that the bombing was the work of the Al-Qaeda terrorist network.

Answers on page 185.

A Russian Named Zubilin

ACCUSED	FACTORIES	PREPARED
AFTER	HEADQUARTERS	REASON
AMERICA	INDUSTRIAL	RECEIVE
ANONYMOUS	INTRIGUE	SABOTAGE
ATTEMPT	MAJOR	SIGNIFICANT
CLOSER	MATERIAL	TOWNS
COAST	MONEY	TYPEWRITTEN
CONVINCE	PARTNER	UNBELIEVABLE
COUNTRY	PIQUED	VITAL
COWARD	POTENTIAL	YEARS
EXTENT	PREDICATE	

The United States and Russia were allies during World War II, and the idea that Russia might send spies to the U.S. wasn't a concern to the FBI. So when they received an anonymous letter written in Russian in 1943, the agency was curious. After translating the message into English, they were not only curious, but surprised, as well.

S	A	B	O	T	A	G	E	B	R	E	S	O	L	C	M	P
L	F	K	M	Z	L	A	I	T	N	E	T	O	P	H	U	I
A	T	R	L	S	I	G	N	I	F	I	C	A	N	T	N	Q
T	S	P	Z	U	U	L	O	E	C	N	I	V	N	O	C	U
I	A	W	M	R	E	A	S	O	N	Q	R	E	T	F	A	E
V	O	S	R	E	T	R	A	U	Q	D	A	E	H	C	U	D
T	C	P	Q	J	T	P	S	D	O	E	M	N	K	N	Q	L
Y	B	R	P	A	D	T	R	E	U	M	Q	A	B	R	A	B
P	T	E	P	O	M	A	A	G	I	P	Y	E	J	I	T	R
E	D	P	R	A	W	E	I	L	R	R	L	N	R	O	R	E
W	E	A	G	O	R	R	R	E	E	I	O	T	O	T	R	C
R	S	R	C	U	T	T	D	I	E	X	S	T	O	N	Q	E
I	U	E	Y	N	Y	I	N	V	C	U	T	W	C	R	A	I
T	C	D	I	E	C	U	A	E	D	A	N	E	W	A	O	V
T	C	X	N	A	A	B	L	N	R	S	M	N	N	I	F	E
E	A	O	T	C	L	R	I	J	L	A	I	R	E	T	A	M
N	M	E	F	E	Y	T	S	C	O	U	N	T	R	Y	L	H

The author of the letter claimed that at least ten Soviet diplomats in the U.S., including the Second Secretary of the Soviet Embassy in Washington, Vasilli Zubilin, were spies. An investigation confirmed the letter's accusations, and the FBI began preparing itself for the coming Cold War.

Answers on page 186.

The End of Baby Face

AMMUNITION	GUN	SMUGGLINGS
ASSOCIATES	HOODLUMS	STILLS
AUTOMATIC	ILLINOIS	TEENS
BATTLE	INJURED	TRACED
BOOTLEGGING	INSPECTOR	TRANSPORT
CONNECTIONS	JUVENILE	TRUCK
FLED	LIQUOR	UNDERWORLD
FORCES	LIVED	VEHICLE
GANGSTERS	NORTHERN	WITNESS
GOVERNMENT	RETURNED	WOUNDED
GROUP	ROBBERY	

Lester Gillis—better known as "Baby Face" Nelson due to his young appearance and small stature—met John Paul Chase in 1932. The two career criminals became fast friends and eventually joined up with the notorious Dillinger gang. Throughout their life of crime, the duo robbed banks and murdered numerous people. The FBI caught up with them in 1934, engaging in a car chase and gun fight with Nelson and Chase.

B	D	E	V	I	L	S	S	E	N	T	I	W	E	H	H	I
C	E	W	S	G	N	I	L	G	G	U	M	S	S	S	J	I
H	B	A	U	Q	V	U	I	P	B	Y	F	E	W	E	V	S
G	N	M	N	N	K	E	U	N	R	A	T	L	C	X	I	G
W	A	M	O	O	D	O	L	E	S	A	T	O	E	O	V	T
O	U	U	R	M	R	E	B	I	I	P	N	T	N	D	R	T
U	T	N	T	G	R	B	R	C	N	N	E	I	L	A	D	N
N	O	I	H	V	O	O	O	W	E	E	L	C	N	E	E	E
D	M	T	E	R	E	S	U	C	O	L	V	S	T	Q	C	M
E	A	I	R	N	S	H	T	Q	I	R	P	U	N	O	A	N
D	T	O	N	A	T	I	I	S	I	O	L	U	J	O	R	R
D	I	N	W	R	O	X	A	C	R	L	G	D	H	J	T	E
U	C	O	U	N	B	O	O	T	L	E	G	G	I	N	G	V
A	T	C	S	Q	K	F	O	R	C	E	S	K	U	N	D	O
W	K	S	N	E	E	T	G	A	N	G	S	T	E	R	S	G
D	E	N	R	U	T	E	R	C	S	L	L	I	T	S	M	T
T	D	D	E	R	U	J	N	I	S	M	U	L	D	O	O	H

Two agents were killed, and Nelson was critically injured, dying that evening. Chase was arrested a month later and became the first person tried under the law making it a federal crime to murder an FBI agent.

Answers on page 186.

German Spy Roundup

ACCIDENT	FINALLY	NONE
AGENT	FOLLOW	NOTEBOOK
ASSIGNMENTS	INDUSTRIOUS	OTHER
BATTLE	INFORMATION	RING
CAPTAIN	INTERCEPTED	SENTENCED
CAPTURE	JAIL	SPY
CASE	JAYWALKER	TRACKED
CENSORS	LEADS	TROOPS
COMPANION	MANUFACTURING	VITAL
DELIGHTED	MOTION	YOUNG
DESCRIBED	MYSTERIOUS	

When a man was hit and killed by a taxi in New York City in 1941, his companion did a strange thing. Instead of calling for help, he grabbed the man's attaché case and fled the scene. Discovering that the victim possessed documents written in German and information about U.S. soldiers, the NYPD contacted the FBI.

V	J	S	S	E	N	T	E	N	C	E	D	N	T	M	I	E
Z	E	U	N	I	A	T	P	A	C	M	O	N	G	A	N	S
C	N	O	J	R	D	H	P	O	Z	N	E	M	N	N	T	P
O	O	I	Z	T	H	T	E	V	E	G	N	B	I	U	E	Y
C	I	R	K	Z	U	C	S	H	A	Y	B	W	R	F	R	Z
E	N	T	T	R	N	O	T	E	B	O	O	K	G	A	C	S
N	A	S	E	L	D	E	B	I	R	C	S	E	D	C	E	T
S	P	U	D	S	A	N	D	E	K	C	A	R	T	T	P	N
O	M	D	J	T	U	T	O	E	Z	O	Y	Y	Y	U	T	E
R	O	N	R	A	A	O	I	I	T	E	C	O	P	R	E	M
S	C	I	I	L	I	C	I	V	T	H	L	A	U	I	D	N
O	B	C	A	S	E	L	C	R	F	O	G	T	R	N	O	G
T	G	O	L	E	A	D	S	I	E	O	M	I	T	G	G	I
H	S	P	O	O	R	T	M	H	D	T	L	Z	L	A	J	S
E	R	E	K	L	A	W	Y	A	J	E	S	L	G	E	B	S
R	I	F	I	N	A	L	L	Y	M	X	N	Y	O	G	D	A
D	I	N	F	O	R	M	A	T	I	O	N	T	M	W	S	Z

Agents were able to ascertain that the victim's companion was American-born Kurt Frederick Ludwig, who had moved to Germany as a young man. There, he was recruited to act as a spy against his birth country. By 1946, the FBI tracked and arrested every member of Ludwig's spy ring.

 Answers on page 186.

The Two Colonels

ALTERNATE	FORCE	QUARTERS
ARMY	FRONT	REMARK
BRIEFCASE	HOUSE	RENDEZVOUS
CASH	LOUNGE	REPLIED
CIVILIAN	MUSTACHE	RUDDY
COFFEE	NEWCOMER	SIDE
COLONEL	OFFICER	SOVIET
DELEGATION	PARTY	STATEMENT
DRIVER	PLACE	STREET
EYEBROWS	PREARRANGE	TWEED
FALSE	PROPOSAL	

In 1954 in East Berlin, an American Army colonel met up with a Soviet acquaintance who had an unusual request. The Soviet asked if the colonel could travel to New York City after his return to the U.S. and provide a contact with some information about the U.S. Army.

E	H	O	R	E	M	O	C	W	E	N	B	Q	S	A	F	D
M	E	F	E	S	U	R	L	Q	U	A	R	T	E	R	S	I
S	S	F	H	T	S	C	O	L	O	N	E	L	V	J	X	P
O	A	I	C	A	F	U	A	L	T	E	R	N	A	T	E	R
V	C	C	A	T	L	G	O	H	S	A	C	R	V	W	N	O
I	F	E	T	E	A	E	O	V	D	C	E	D	P	R	A	P
E	E	R	S	M	G	S	E	E	Z	P	P	A	F	E	I	O
T	I	M	U	E	H	N	L	F	L	E	R	Z	O	V	L	S
R	R	D	M	N	J	E	U	I	F	T	D	D	R	I	I	A
N	B	X	A	T	G	Q	E	O	Y	O	P	N	C	R	V	L
V	R	L	Z	A	M	D	A	F	L	K	C	N	E	D	I	X
E	Q	U	T	E	G	N	A	R	R	A	E	R	P	R	C	T
V	S	I	D	O	S	W	O	R	B	E	Y	E	W	L	E	R
W	O	L	S	D	T	W	E	E	D	S	X	E	A	E	R	P
N	F	I	A	T	Y	T	N	O	R	F	K	M	R	R	S	N
N	D	E	I	F	R	K	R	A	M	E	R	T	E	A	M	Q
E	C	A	L	P	R	H	O	U	S	E	S	D	K	F	V	Y

The colonel immediately relayed the details of this meeting to the FBI, who came up with a plan. Instead of the colonel, an FBI agent lookalike would meet the Soviet contact in New York. The ruse worked, and the contact, a United Nations Soviet delegate named Maksim Martynov, was identified. Martynov returned to the Soviet Union and was barred from entering the U.S. again.

Answers on page 186.

Guenther Rumrich

AGENTS	ESPIONAGE	PROSECUTION
BRIBE	EXPOSED	SQUARELY
CASE	FIRED	STAGED
CHARGE	FISHES	TAMPERING
CITIZEN	FLAWED	TESTIMONY
COORDINATION	FOREIGN	TOOLS
CORROBORATE	INTERNATIONAL	TRAINED
CRIMINAL	LOOMING	ULTIMATELY
DESPITE	MAJOR	UNPREPARED
EFFECTIVE	OPERATING	WRITE
ENVIRONMENT	OVERZEALOUS	

Even before the United States entered World War II, Nazi spies were working in the country. But the FBI wasn't used to investigating such matters, and their first espionage case was a learning experience. It began when naturalized U.S. citizen Guenther Rumrich was caught attempting to procure blank passports for Nazi agents.

C	F	Y	S	E	K	Y	L	E	T	A	M	I	T	L	U	T
S	I	L	U	N	P	R	E	P	A	R	E	D	E	M	B	O
L	T	T	A	I	C	T	S	G	D	W	L	C	F	A	K	O
O	D	N	I	W	B	R	Q	N	E	E	I	H	F	R	L	L
V	M	E	E	Z	E	B	U	I	S	T	N	A	E	O	A	S
E	P	M	G	G	E	D	A	T	O	I	T	R	C	O	N	G
R	N	N	C	A	A	N	R	A	P	P	E	G	T	O	I	N
Z	W	O	L	O	T	V	E	R	X	S	R	E	I	Y	M	I
E	N	R	I	T	R	S	L	E	E	E	N	T	V	T	I	R
A	G	I	V	T	Z	R	Y	P	R	D	A	J	E	E	R	E
L	I	V	B	E	U	T	O	O	L	N	T	F	S	S	C	P
O	E	N	A	S	R	C	J	B	I	O	I	N	V	T	B	M
U	R	E	X	A	C	A	E	D	O	R	O	E	W	I	R	A
S	O	W	I	C	M	Y	R	S	E	R	N	M	R	M	I	T
D	F	N	A	H	N	O	T	D	O	C	A	N	I	O	B	D
Y	E	S	P	I	O	N	A	G	E	R	L	T	T	N	E	Y
D	J	S	L	C	S	E	H	S	I	F	P	G	E	Y	G	J

In exchange for a lesser sentence, Rumrich offered up names of Nazi spies. But the agent in charge botched the investigation, allowing many spies to flee before apprehension. The case resulted in reformed procedures for espionage incidents, which were later used in the 1941 Duquesne Spy Ring case.

 Answers on page 187.

Corruption Waltzes Out

ALLEGATIONS
BAGMEN
BENEFIT
BRIBERY
COLLEAGUES
COMMISSION
CONTRACTOR
DRAFTED
EMPLOYEE
EQUIPMENT
ETHICS
EXAMPLES
FICTITIOUS
INDEPENDENT
INVOICE
JUSTICE
JUVENILE
LANDMARK
LAWMAKERS
LEGISLATURE
LOBBYIST
OFFICIALS
ONE
PUBLIC
RECORD
SCAM
SIX
SONG
SPUR
SYSTEMIC
UGLY
WRONGDOING

In 2002, the FBI office in Memphis received reports of fraud in the Juvenile Court Clerk's Office. During the course of the investigation, wrongdoing was uncovered not only in local government, but also in the state legislature.

L	J	L	B	C	E	M	P	L	O	Y	E	E	Q	Q	Z	N
E	C	O	L	L	E	A	G	U	E	S	H	S	K	L	H	H
G	T	B	S	W	E	S	O	F	F	I	C	I	A	L	S	L
I	I	B	S	I	R	N	B	B	N	I	Z	N	S	F	I	S
S	W	Y	G	Y	X	O	R	V	H	E	D	Y	E	N	N	E
L	R	I	Z	T	S	I	N	T	E	M	M	C	A	O	R	L
A	O	S	P	R	B	T	E	G	A	C	I	G	I	X	T	P
T	T	T	S	E	R	A	E	R	D	O	I	S	A	N	O	M
U	C	N	R	E	U	G	K	M	V	O	S	T	E	B	N	A
R	A	Y	E	Q	P	E	E	N	I	I	I	D	S	V	L	X
E	R	N	K	U	S	L	I	S	M	C	N	N	S	U	C	E
A	T	W	A	I	A	L	F	M	I	E	Y	L	G	U	J	F
Q	N	P	M	P	O	A	O	L	P	T	I	F	E	N	E	B
N	O	S	W	M	N	C	B	E	S	D	R	O	C	E	R	T
M	C	C	A	E	E	U	D	O	D	E	T	F	A	R	D	L
K	L	A	L	N	P	N	N	E	L	I	N	E	V	U	J	N
D	L	M	Q	T	I	G	S	U	O	I	T	I	T	C	I	F

In an undercover operation known as Tennessee Waltz, agents set up a fake company that was said to provide electronic equipment to third world countries, then requested legislation that would benefit the "company." Undercover agents recorded politicians taking bribes in exchange for favorable votes or legislation, and by 2008, 12 officials, including state senators, had been arrested for corruption.

 Answers on page 187.

The Touhy Gang

ACCOUNTED
BOMB
CHANCE
CONVOY
DEAD
DRIVER
EVIDENCE
FARM
FLAG
FOREST
GANG
GARBAGE
GRAPEVINE
HOSTAGES
MANNED
MEDIUM
MEMBERS
MOBSTERS
NEGOTIATIONS
PATROLMAN
PLAN
PUNCTUAL
RANSOM
SHABBY
SHIFT
SMASHED
TERRITORY
TRUSTY
TWO
UNDERWORLD
VICTIM

The United States was at war in 1942, and the Selective Service Act required all men of a certain age to register for military service. So when a group of criminals, including Roger "The Terrible" Touhy and Basil "The Owl" Banghart, escaped from a Joliet, Illinois, prison that year and failed to register, the FBI had a legal reason to get involved in their manhunt.

L	N	E	G	O	T	I	A	T	I	O	N	S	Y	F	L	O
S	X	D	G	A	L	F	U	R	Y	D	A	S	D	B	T	W
Y	Q	D	N	N	C	E	E	W	E	W	H	R	U	A	G	T
H	E	E	Q	M	A	V	P	T	V	W	N	E	N	Y	S	T
D	E	N	O	C	I	M	N	A	F	T	A	B	D	S	M	B
H	N	N	Q	R	O	U	L	R	C	O	L	M	E	H	A	P
O	I	A	D	M	O	N	A	O	K	A	P	E	R	I	S	B
S	V	M	A	C	O	N	V	P	R	M	S	M	W	F	H	C
T	E	B	C	T	S	B	U	O	U	T	L	E	O	T	E	H
A	P	A	F	O	E	N	S	I	Y	M	A	M	R	U	D	A
G	A	Z	M	M	C	R	D	T	M	F	Y	P	L	G	Y	N
E	R	V	O	T	K	E	R	F	E	I	M	R	D	O	B	C
S	G	A	U	J	M	D	O	I	K	R	T	R	Q	G	B	E
G	Y	A	C	A	V	R	P	B	T	D	S	C	A	G	A	N
A	L	E	C	N	E	D	I	V	E	O	E	H	I	F	H	T
N	T	R	U	S	T	Y	E	G	A	B	R	A	G	V	S	K
G	D	E	T	W	P	T	B	O	M	B	L	Y	D	Q	Q	D

The gang thought they had been careful to not break any federal laws, wanting to keep the FBI off their trail. But they forgot about the Selective Service law, and soon J. Edgar Hoover himself had Touhy, Banghart, and rest of the gang in custody.

Answers on page 187.

The Morris Worm

ANONYMOUS	EXACT	MALICIOUSLY
BRIEF	EXPERTS	NETWORK
CASUALTIES	FEDERAL	PRIVATE
CLEVER	FEVERISHLY	PROPAGATE
CULPRIT	FINGER	PUBLIC
CYBER	HACKERS	SOFTWARE
DAMAGES	HARMLESS	SPLASH
DESTROY	HIDDEN	VIRUSES
DIGITAL	INCRIMINATING	VULNERABLE
EMERGENCY	INDICTED	WORM
EVIDENCE	INNOVATOR	

In 1988, only about 60,000 computers were connected to the internet. And in November of that year, a cyber worm made its way through 6,000 of those computers. Although not terribly malicious, the worm slowed vital functions to a crawl and left users struggling for a fix. The FBI launched an investigation, soon identifying graduate student Robert Tappan Morris as the originator of the worm.

S	S	S	E	L	M	R	A	H	R	H	A	C	K	E	R	S
T	G	W	H	D	E	T	C	I	D	N	I	N	C	I	E	M
R	S	E	M	E	R	G	E	N	C	Y	U	S	I	N	V	A
E	S	R	O	T	A	V	O	N	N	I	M	U	L	C	I	L
P	E	T	A	G	A	P	O	R	P	X	X	O	B	R	D	I
X	S	S	E	I	T	L	A	U	S	A	C	M	U	I	E	C
E	U	V	V	D	E	C	N	H	X	B	S	Y	P	M	N	I
A	R	U	G	F	L	T	I	V	M	H	N	N	C	I	C	O
U	I	L	W	E	E	D	A	F	R	E	K	O	Y	N	E	U
L	V	N	V	O	D	I	I	V	T	D	X	N	B	A	T	S
Y	A	E	J	E	R	N	R	W	I	S	A	A	E	T	I	L
O	R	R	N	W	G	M	O	B	P	R	K	M	R	I	R	Y
R	J	A	E	E	Z	R	O	L	H	K	P	E	A	N	X	Z
T	K	B	R	D	K	L	A	T	I	G	I	D	X	G	F	E
S	Q	L	V	Z	E	S	C	U	L	P	R	I	T	A	E	Q
E	Z	E	X	J	H	F	E	R	A	W	T	F	O	S	C	S
D	N	Y	L	H	S	I	R	E	V	E	F	C	M	P	P	T

Morris admitted to the attack but claimed it was an accident, even providing instructions for the removal of the program. Accident or not, the worm revealed the vulnerabilities of the internet and resulted in the creation of the country's first computer emergency response team.

 Answers on page 187.

Alfred Brady and the Gang

ACTIVITIES	DROVE	MOOT
AMMUNITION	ESCAPE	MURDER
BANDIT	FATE	PART
BARROOM	GANG	PROSECUTIVE
BLOODTHIRSTY	HOLDUPS	ROBBING
CHARGE	INSTITUTION	STEPFATHER
COALITION	JEWELRY	STOLEN
CRAZY	JURISDICTION	VAGRANCY
CRIMINAL	LATTER	VIOLATIONS
DEPREDATIONS	MANNER	WELDER
DESPERADOES	MEMBERS	

Alfred Brady and his cohorts, James Dalhover and Clarence Lee Shaffer Jr., made a career of robbing stores and banks, racking up about 150 holdups by 1936. The gang, who owned dozens of firearms, traveled to Bangor, Maine, in the fall of 1937 to add to their collection. But the FBI, already tipped off to their criminal activity, was waiting for them in a sporting goods store.

I	F	G	S	N	O	I	T	A	D	E	R	P	E	D	J	N
Y	U	A	M	M	U	N	I	T	I	O	N	E	V	O	R	D
R	D	N	T	G	N	I	B	B	O	R	D	T	X	Y	I	A
L	E	G	Q	E	R	E	T	T	A	L	T	R	L	T	P	C
E	S	H	O	L	D	U	P	S	X	N	I	A	N	S	X	O
W	P	H	W	E	L	D	E	R	S	N	N	O	S	R	R	A
E	E	T	I	D	N	A	B	T	S	I	I	S	N	I	E	L
J	R	H	N	I	J	Y	E	T	M	T	E	M	O	H	N	I
D	A	H	H	I	Z	P	I	I	C	I	E	Y	I	T	N	T
T	D	Y	H	A	F	T	R	I	T	M	M	C	T	D	A	I
N	O	A	R	A	U	C	D	I	B	O	M	N	A	O	M	O
C	E	C	T	T	E	S	V	E	O	M	E	A	L	O	A	N
H	S	H	I	S	I	I	R	R	U	L	P	R	O	L	G	W
A	E	O	C	R	T	S	R	R	O	A	D	G	I	B	R	L
R	N	A	U	C	N	A	D	T	R	F	E	A	V	B	H	Y
G	P	J	A	H	B	E	S	T	Z	R	Y	V	Q	X	T	I
E	M	O	O	T	R	P	R	O	S	E	C	U	T	I	V	E

Dalhover was immediately apprehended when he entered the store, but Brady and Shaffer chose to fight, firing their guns at agents. The two criminals died in the gunfight, and Dalhover, found guilty of murdering a police officer, was executed in 1938.

 Answers on page 188.

Making a Racket

ACUMEN	FLAIR	PLEAS
APATHETIC	FUGITIVE	PROTECTIVE
BRICKBATS	GARB	PROVISIONS
BRUTALITY	HAPHAZARD	RACKETEERS
COMMUNICATION	INTIMIDATION	RESTRAIN
CONSPIRACY	JAIL	SECRETLY
CULMINATE	JUSTICE	STENCH
DEALERS	MANDATES	TRIBUTE
EMPIRE	MANHUNT	UNIONS
EXPERIENCE	METROPOLITAN	VAGARIES
EXTORTION	PENAL	

In the 1930s, the racketeering activities of Jacob Shapiro and Louis Buchalter influenced the fur industry in New York. The two gangsters led an underworld empire that controlled the business dealings of dozens of fur dressers and intimidated those who refused to cooperate with their demands. The pair organized at least 10 bombings, one kidnapping, and two cases of arson.

J	O	C	H	R	A	C	K	E	T	E	E	R	S	C	N	S
C	O	O	J	U	S	T	I	C	E	S	E	S	O	A	W	N
H	O	N	A	R	X	E	Q	E	T	T	E	M	T	Y	E	O
W	S	S	P	E	L	A	M	E	U	C	M	I	S	T	X	I
S	T	P	A	S	D	P	N	B	R	U	L	E	R	I	T	S
E	A	I	T	T	I	C	I	E	N	O	E	V	E	L	O	I
T	B	R	H	R	H	R	T	I	P	X	M	I	L	A	R	V
A	K	A	E	A	T	L	C	O	P	A	R	T	A	T	T	O
D	C	C	T	I	Y	A	R	E	N	I	L	I	E	U	I	R
N	I	Y	I	N	T	T	R	H	A	I	C	G	D	R	O	P
A	R	D	C	I	E	I	U	L	A	L	I	U	D	B	N	S
M	B	U	O	M	E	N	F	J	J	P	D	F	G	T	N	N
S	L	N	I	N	T	I	M	I	D	A	T	I	O	N	E	O
A	A	Y	C	E	E	T	A	N	I	M	L	U	C	K	M	I
E	N	E	X	O	N	H	A	P	H	A	Z	A	R	D	U	N
L	E	E	E	V	I	T	C	E	T	O	R	P	Z	F	C	U
P	P	Q	H	O	S	E	I	R	A	G	A	V	B	R	A	G

By 1937, the FBI had arrested both men, but after being released on bond they skipped town and were declared fugitives. Each succumbed to a guilty conscience, however, with Shapiro turning himself in 1938 and Buchalter following suit in 1939.

Answers on page 188.

Sabotage in Zambia

ABORT	DYNAMITE	PURCHASE
ALIBI	GUISE	RAILROAD
AUTHORITIES	HARDWARE	SENTENCE
BRIDGE	INTERRUPT	SERVICE
CHIEF	LOBBY	TESTIFY
CLOCKS	LOSS	TIME
CONDITIONS	MARKET	TRAVEL
COOPERATE	NATURALIZED	UPSWING
COPPER	PAYMENT	VISAS
CUSTOMS	PLEASURE	WORK
DESTROY	PROBATION	

In 1966, the FBI learned that several Americans were plotting to blow up a railroad bridge in the Republic of Zambia. The question was, why would Americans want to attack a peaceful foreign nation? The answer was discovered after interviewing the culprits, all of whom worked in the copper industry.

S	C	P	R	O	B	A	T	I	O	N	C	D	Z	L	Z	U
N	O	E	S	S	O	L	D	T	M	O	E	B	Y	F	P	T
W	O	R	O	V	B	T	T	A	N	Z	O	Z	Y	S	U	P
L	P	U	O	K	I	R	R	D	I	E	V	O	W	E	R	U
O	E	S	K	M	A	K	I	L	A	N	M	I	U	Z	C	R
Y	R	A	Q	V	E	T	A	E	B	Y	N	Y	F	C	H	R
O	A	E	E	T	I	R	E	G	O	G	G	F	A	S	A	E
R	T	L	S	O	U	C	D	D	R	C	P	A	E	P	S	T
T	E	P	N	T	N	Y	S	I	T	I	O	I	L	I	E	N
S	G	S	A	E	N	M	M	R	P	E	T	P	R	I	H	I
E	I	N	T	A	O	S	T	B	R	I	P	A	P	L	B	C
D	B	N	M	T	E	E	S	A	R	Y	I	L	R	E	V	I
W	E	I	S	R	S	A	W	O	Q	L	B	B	Z	O	R	G
S	T	U	V	T	S	D	H	G	R	H	I	B	T	K	I	U
E	C	I	I	I	R	T	V	O	C	W	O	U	O	I	R	I
C	C	F	V	A	U	S	A	K	R	O	W	N	R	L	M	S
E	Y	E	H	A	A	D	S	S	K	C	O	L	C	U	J	E

As one of the leading producers of copper in the world, Zambia relied on railroads to ship the metal. By blowing up the railroad, the country's copper supply would be disrupted, leading to financial gains in other parts of the world. Fortunately, the plan was thwarted, and the saboteurs were arrested, fined, and jailed.

Answers on page 188.

The Osage Indian Murders

BOMBED	FOUR	POWER
BRIBED	FRAUD	PRIVATE
BULLET	HENCHMEN	PROSPECTOR
CONNECTION	HERBAL	RAVINE
CREATIVE	HIRED	ROYALTIES
CROOKED	INHERIT	SISTERS
DECOMPOSED	KILLER	SLEW
DISTRUSTFUL	LAWYER	UNDERTAKER
DOCTOR	LIED	WEALTH
FALSE	LOCALS	WHERE
FAMILY	MATTER	

In the early 1920s, a rash of mysterious murders terrorized the Osage Native American community in Oklahoma. Anna Brown and four members of her family were killed, followed by several other victims. Many suspected William Hale, a local cattleman determined to gain rights to the oil on Osage land.

B	I	A	Y	E	T	A	V	I	R	P	V	D	I	D	G	C
A	N	K	A	C	S	L	A	C	O	L	E	N	M	U	U	R
W	H	E	R	E	W	R	I	H	L	B	R	A	T	A	B	E
N	E	M	H	C	N	E	H	A	M	O	T	D	Z	R	N	A
R	R	Y	E	L	R	G	U	O	T	T	E	D	S	F	O	T
D	I	P	K	P	U	S	B	C	E	I	E	D	R	L	I	I
E	T	O	T	W	O	M	E	R	L	B	I	D	E	A	T	V
C	T	W	U	U	F	P	O	I	I	S	E	D	T	W	C	E
O	E	E	G	N	S	J	F	R	T	K	V	T	S	Y	E	Q
M	L	R	A	O	D	K	B	R	O	L	Y	I	I	E	N	U
P	L	D	R	L	I	E	U	O	F	U	A	V	S	R	N	K
O	U	P	O	L	M	S	R	E	H	A	P	Y	Q	Y	O	H
S	B	A	L	C	T	C	Q	T	N	T	M	E	O	U	C	I
E	F	E	N	F	T	H	S	N	A	I	L	I	S	R	H	R
D	R	G	U	V	H	O	W	L	W	K	V	A	L	L	C	E
B	D	L	B	G	A	V	R	P	E	P	E	A	E	Y	A	D
F	U	H	E	R	B	A	L	W	A	W	R	R	R	W	X	F

In fact, Hale's nephew had been married to Anna's sister, and the connection meant that control of the oil could pass to Hale—if Anna's entire family, and anyone else who got in his way, was dead. To catch the killer, four FBI agents went undercover and built a solid case against Hale, who was convicted of murder in 1929.

Answers on page 188.

Nazi Saboteurs in America

ASHORE	EUPHORIC	NAVAL
BEACH	EXPLOSIVES	PENALTY
BRIBE	FORCES	PRIMER
CLAD	FURNISHED	PRODUCTION
COMMISSION	INCENDIARIES	RESOLUTION
CUSTODY	INTERROGATED	SABOTAGE
DESPERATE	INVASIONS	TECHNIQUES
DIMINISH	MAGNESIUM	TRAIN
DISCHARGE	MAJOR	UNIFORMS
DISRUPTION	MIDNIGHT	VITAL
EQUIPMENT	MOTIVE	

On June 19, 1942, a man called FBI Headquarters in Washington D.C. and told a shocking story. The man, German-born George Dasch, confessed to being part of a group of saboteurs. Mere days earlier, two Nazi submarines landed in New York and Florida, full of explosives and incendiary devices. The men on board the subs were prepared for a years-long mission of sabotage, intending to disrupt American military manufacturing.

R	E	E	U	P	N	O	I	S	S	I	M	M	O	C	N	J
E	B	Y	V	D	I	Y	T	L	A	N	E	P	E	W	E	H
M	I	D	N	I	N	J	D	F	A	U	K	G	X	D	T	L
I	R	O	I	S	T	N	N	E	U	S	A	F	I	A	A	Q
R	B	T	A	R	E	O	O	T	H	T	H	M	Y	L	R	O
P	M	S	R	U	R	T	M	I	O	S	I	O	S	C	E	S
Z	U	U	T	P	R	M	N	B	T	N	I	E	R	R	P	E
R	I	C	S	T	O	D	A	E	I	C	I	N	E	E	S	U
I	S	E	M	I	G	S	I	S	M	R	U	S	R	G	E	Q
N	E	U	R	O	A	L	H	S	A	P	O	D	T	U	D	I
V	N	P	O	N	T	O	A	I	C	L	I	H	O	F	F	N
A	G	H	F	B	E	N	D	T	U	H	G	U	O	R	M	H
S	A	O	I	E	D	N	A	T	I	I	A	R	Q	A	P	C
I	M	R	N	A	E	L	I	V	N	V	C	R	J	E	A	E
O	C	I	U	C	V	O	E	D	A	E	V	O	G	B	H	T
N	E	C	N	H	N	Z	I	K	S	L	R	I	M	E	E	X
S	D	I	I	W	T	M	E	X	P	L	O	S	I	V	E	S

Luckily, Dasch got cold feet and turned himself in, giving the FBI information to catch the remaining saboteurs. Although originally sentenced to death, Dasch was granted clemency by President Truman in 1948 and returned to Germany.

 Answers on page 189.

The Elizabeth Short Murder

ARMY	HOPEFUL	NEIGHBORHOOD
AUTHORITIES	KILLER	POSED
BODY	LOBBY	PRINTS
CHECKS	MANNEQUIN	RECORDS
CHILD	MINUTES	SHEER
CLEANLY	MORNING	SKILLS
COMMISSARY	MOTHER	STUDENTS
CONDUCTED	MUG	TAKING
DISSECTION	MUTILATION	TANTALIZING
FINGERPRINTS	MYSTERY	WAIST
GRUESOME	NAKED	

It's a case that still mystifies professional investigators and amateur sleuths alike: A young woman, found mutilated and murdered in a Los Angeles neighborhood on January 15, 1947, without a drop of blood nearby. Although few clues were found to point toward a culprit, the FBI was able to identify the body within just 56 minutes, thanks to fingerprint technology.

W	Q	P	E	F	I	N	G	E	R	P	R	I	N	T	S	S
N	O	I	T	A	L	I	T	U	M	R	E	L	L	I	K	O
M	U	M	D	N	S	F	E	C	H	E	C	K	S	U	M	S
O	D	V	Z	E	E	D	K	M	Y	S	T	E	R	Y	A	T
T	E	S	E	I	T	I	R	O	H	T	U	A	E	U	N	U
H	K	L	G	G	I	C	G	O	P	C	C	W	E	U	N	D
E	A	L	N	D	R	C	U	H	C	N	E	A	H	C	E	E
R	N	I	I	Y	S	U	L	D	B	E	I	I	S	H	Q	N
Y	U	K	Z	R	E	L	E	J	N	O	R	S	Q	I	U	T
I	M	S	I	A	T	J	U	S	C	O	R	T	D	L	I	S
T	P	R	L	S	U	I	D	F	O	L	C	H	M	D	N	M
A	R	T	A	S	N	J	E	A	E	M	E	N	O	Z	M	P
K	I	I	T	I	I	G	S	J	D	P	E	A	N	O	L	F
I	N	P	N	M	M	U	O	O	K	D	O	A	N	O	D	B
N	T	L	A	M	R	M	P	H	R	C	C	H	B	L	O	K
G	S	K	T	O	M	O	R	N	I	N	G	B	P	D	Y	T
N	O	I	T	C	E	S	S	I	D	N	Y	K	Y	Y	B	M

The woman, 22-year-old Elizabeth Short—quickly dubbed the "Black Dahlia" by the press—had been fingerprinted for a job with the Army and also after being arrested for underage drinking. But while the Black Dahlia was quickly identified, the identity of her murderer remains a mystery.

 Answers on page 189.

Operation Innocent Images

ACTIVITIES	HOMES	ORIGINAL
BOY	ILLICIT	PREDATORS
BULLETIN	IMAGES	RING
COMMERCIAL	IMPRESSIVE	SHARING
DISAPPEARANCE	INCALCULABLE	STUNNED
ELECTRONIC	INITIATIVE	SUPPORT
EVENTS	IRATE	TASK
EXPLOITATION	KIDNAPPING	TECHNIQUES
GIFTS	LINK	UNDERCOVER
GLOBAL	LOCAL	VACATION
GRAPHIC	MISSING	

When a ten-year-old boy went missing from his Brentwood, Maryland, home in May 1993, it sparked the beginning of a new FBI initiative called Operation Innocent Images. During their search for the boy, agents discovered a pair of pedophiles living in the neighborhood who had been using online chat rooms to lure children and to contact other child predators.

Q	E	P	K	U	I	L	L	I	C	I	T	O	Z	S	M	H
I	C	C	B	A	O	K	L	L	S	K	E	F	I	R	I	O
N	O	D	N	V	A	O	I	T	A	X	S	M	F	O	S	M
I	M	S	P	A	C	C	U	D	P	N	P	A	C	T	S	E
T	M	G	E	A	R	N	T	L	N	R	I	I	T	A	I	S
I	E	L	L	U	N	A	O	I	E	A	N	G	T	D	N	G
A	R	O	G	E	Q	I	E	S	V	O	P	R	I	E	G	R
T	C	B	D	R	T	I	S	P	R	I	O	P	S	R	H	E
I	I	A	K	A	A	I	N	T	P	P	T	T	I	P	O	V
V	A	L	T	K	V	P	C	H	P	A	F	I	S	N	I	O
E	L	I	R	E	D	E	H	U	C	I	S	L	E	H	G	C
N	O	B	T	T	L	V	S	I	G	E	I	I	I	S	I	R
N	B	O	Y	E	T	A	R	I	C	Y	T	M	D	N	N	E
G	F	W	V	A	C	A	T	I	O	N	F	X	A	M	K	D
N	E	L	B	A	L	U	C	L	A	C	N	I	Z	G	K	N
I	E	V	E	N	T	S	G	N	I	R	A	H	S	A	E	U
R	J	P	I	U	N	I	T	E	L	L	U	B	K	G	Y	S

FBI agents posed undercover as children, to converse with these predators and arrest them, breaking up networks of pedophiles and stopping them from distributing child pornography. Sadly, the missing boy was never found; but the FBI continues to work tirelessly for the innocent victims of exploitation.

 Answers on page 189.

Mortgage Fraud Takedown

ADDRESS	FISCAL	MARKET
ANALYSTS	FLIPPING	MORTGAGE
APPRAISERS	FRAUD	ORIGINATION
ARTIFICIAL	GROWING	OVERALL
BUYERS	HIGHLIGHT	PARTICIPATE
COMBAT	HOUSING	SCHEMES
COMMUNITIES	IMPACT	SHORT
DEVASTATES	INDUSTRY	TAKEDOWN
ENFORCEMENT	INSIDERS	UNDERCOVER
ESTATE	LOANS	VARIETY
FEDERAL	LOCAL	

Owning a home is often a dream for many Americans. Unfortunately, incidents of criminal activity in the housing industry have ruined lives and shattered the aspirations of many families. Con artists prey upon the hopes of homebuyers by inflating home prices or selling mortgages on properties that don't exist, often targeting immigrants and the elderly.

E	T	A	P	I	C	I	T	R	A	P	T	A	B	M	O	C
F	G	L	L	L	A	R	E	V	O	C	R	E	D	N	U	V
R	N	N	O	D	E	V	A	S	T	A	T	E	S	O	S	A
A	I	A	N	A	L	Y	S	T	S	S	H	O	R	T	R	R
U	W	O	O	X	N	T	A	L	A	C	S	I	F	E	E	I
D	O	L	P	L	R	S	E	Z	A	P	E	N	C	N	Y	E
E	R	A	L	D	L	U	Q	D	F	E	O	O	A	F	U	T
G	G	R	A	D	V	F	D	L	S	I	M	L	P	O	B	Y
A	W	E	C	N	A	R	I	C	T	M	A	E	P	R	T	R
G	T	D	O	M	E	P	H	A	U	I	T	T	R	C	T	T
T	H	E	L	S	P	E	N	N	C	A	E	C	A	E	A	S
R	O	F	S	I	M	I	I	I	T	K	P	P	I	M	K	U
O	U	U	N	E	G	T	F	S	R	V	M	I	S	E	E	D
M	S	G	S	I	I	I	E	A	B	I	B	W	E	N	D	N
A	I	T	R	E	T	O	M	F	C	V	I	T	R	T	O	I
K	N	O	S	R	I	N	S	I	D	E	R	S	S	B	W	U
Q	G	K	A	H	I	G	H	L	I	G	H	T	K	F	N	D

The FBI's Operation Stolen Dreams, launched in 2010, used surveillance and undercover tactics to investigate 3,000 mortgage fraud cases. The operation, which also made use of other federal, state, and local agencies, led to the arrest of 485 people and $11 million in restitution for victims.

 Answers on page 189.

Radical Bombs and the Red Scare

ACTIVITY	DUBBED	PACKAGES
ANARCHISTS	FANFARE	POSTAL
ANXIETY	INVESTIGATE	RADICALS
BLAST	LABOR	ROUNDUP
BOMBING	LAW	SCRAP
BRIGHT	LESSONS	SEDITION
CITIES	LIBERTIES	SHIP
COUNTRY	MAILED	STREET
DEPORTED	MONTH	SUSPECTED
DIVISION	NIGHTMARE	YOUNG
DOMESTIC	OVERZEALOUS	

When an anarchist named Carlo Valdinoci blew up a bomb outside Attorney General A. Mitchell Palmer's house in Washington, D.C., on June 2, 1919, it forced the young Bureau of Investigation (which later became the FBI) to learn more about counterterrorism. The bombing, which killed Valdinoci, was just one in a series of bombings that had targeted politicians, judges, and other officials in eight cities.

F	Y	A	C	R	S	C	S	D	G	W	J	S	I	J	D	R
A	V	C	O	U	G	O	T	H	G	A	N	U	V	N	F	A
N	X	N	A	N	Q	U	S	L	I	L	O	O	Z	Z	Z	D
F	E	G	U	N	R	N	A	A	S	P	I	L	B	F	P	I
A	I	O	N	O	A	T	L	Y	E	H	S	A	A	Q	Q	C
R	Y	M	B	I	S	R	B	P	D	Q	I	E	C	F	I	A
E	I	A	A	O	B	Y	C	E	I	Y	V	Z	T	T	N	L
P	L	N	P	I	A	M	T	H	T	E	I	R	I	H	W	S
A	V	Z	V	W	L	C	O	E	I	O	D	E	V	T	L	E
C	Q	D	B	E	E	E	I	B	O	S	S	V	I	N	I	R
K	P	A	E	P	S	X	D	T	N	E	T	O	T	O	B	A
A	A	B	S	P	N	T	S	H	S	R	H	S	Y	M	E	M
G	B	U	A	A	O	F	I	C	D	E	B	B	U	D	R	T
E	S	T	H	G	I	R	B	G	R	O	M	H	S	D	T	H
S	N	O	S	S	E	L	T	M	A	A	Z	O	N	T	I	G
T	Z	T	E	E	R	T	S	E	J	T	P	C	D	U	E	I
B	E	P	U	D	N	U	O	R	D	W	E	Q	K	T	S	N

Palmer tasked J. Edgar Hoover with leading an investigation, and in 1920, the "Palmer Raids" were launched in an effort to weed out anarchists. Although the raids were widely criticized for being unconstitutional, the Bureau gained valuable insight for future cases.

Answers on page 190.

Pan Am Flight 103

BOUND
CHILL
CHRISTMAS
COLD
COMPLEX
CONSTABLE
COOPERATION
CREW
DEBRIS
DECK
EXPLODED
FORENSIC
FRAGMENTS
GLOBE
GROUND
HOME
IMPACT
INTERNATIONAL
LETHAL
OPERATIVES
PAINSTAKING
PASSENGER
RADIO
SHIRT
SOLVING
SPECIALISTS
SYMBOLIZE
TAPE
THUMBNAIL
TIMER
TRAVERSED
UNPRECEDENTED

Before 9/11, one of the worst acts of terrorism the world had ever seen was the bombing of Pan Am Flight 103 on December 21, 1988. The bombing, which occurred as the plane flew over the town of Lockerbie, Scotland, killed all 259 passengers—including 189 Americans—and 11 people on the ground. The FBI, in conjunction with international investigators, combed over 845 square miles of debris to search for evidence.

P	A	I	N	S	T	A	K	I	N	G	G	H	E	M	O	H
C	O	O	P	E	R	A	T	I	O	N	L	Q	R	L	S	D
A	C	I	S	N	E	R	O	F	U	L	Q	H	S	A	P	E
D	S	R	E	M	I	T	W	C	I	W	R	O	B	N	E	S
E	G	Y	I	D	J	S	O	H	X	E	L	P	M	O	C	R
T	L	M	M	A	E	N	C	Y	E	V	E	L	S	I	I	E
N	O	P	X	B	S	B	A	B	I	D	N	I	A	T	A	V
E	B	Z	A	T	O	F	R	N	K	E	O	A	M	A	L	A
D	E	Y	A	S	B	L	G	I	C	D	I	N	T	N	I	R
E	N	B	T	K	S	O	I	Z	S	O	D	B	S	R	S	T
C	L	U	C	R	E	E	U	Z	Z	L	A	M	I	E	T	C
E	W	E	O	P	I	T	N	N	E	P	R	U	R	T	S	R
R	D	D	A	R	N	H	H	G	D	X	W	H	H	N	A	E
P	L	T	L	I	G	F	S	N	E	E	D	T	C	I	D	W
N	G	B	B	O	K	Y	O	P	E	R	A	T	I	V	E	S
U	I	M	P	A	C	T	L	A	H	T	E	L	T	Z	F	N
A	D	X	S	P	P	F	R	A	G	M	E	N	T	S	Q	H

A tiny piece of a circuit board proved the key to the case, as it led authorities to Libyan intelligence operatives. In 2001, one man was convicted of the bombing, but the FBI continues to search for others who were involved.

 Answers on page 190.

A Front Page Kidnapping

BILLED	EVENING	MAGNATE
BRAINWASH	EXTREMISTS	MEMBERS
BULLETS	FOOD	MILLIONS
BURST	GRABBED	NEWSPAPER
CAUGHT	GUERILLA	PARDONED
CONFEDERATES	GUNS	POWERFUL
CYANIDE	INFORMANTS	RADICALS
DESPITE	HOUSE	TRIAL
DOMESTIC	JOINED	TRUNK
DONATIONS	KNOCK	WOUNDING
DOZEN	LEADS	

On February 4, 1974, a group of armed men and women forced their way into the Berkeley, California, apartment of 19-year-old Patty Hearst, the granddaughter of newspaper magnate William Randolph Hearst. The group, a band of domestic terrorists who called themselves the Symbionese Liberation Army (SLA), kidnapped Hearst and then brainwashed her into joining their cause.

J	D	N	I	N	F	O	R	M	A	N	T	S	D	A	E	L
P	E	C	L	M	E	M	B	E	R	S	C	E	M	D	T	R
A	B	E	C	Y	A	N	I	D	E	O	N	I	O	H	E	E
R	B	K	H	W	V	K	R	G	N	I	L	O	G	I	V	P
D	A	N	O	N	L	B	B	F	O	L	F	U	Z	E	I	A
O	R	U	U	L	X	U	E	J	I	Z	A	F	N	B	W	P
N	G	R	S	T	S	D	F	O	T	C	Q	I	W	U	S	S
E	U	T	E	B	E	N	N	R	S	S	N	U	G	L	A	W
D	X	J	A	R	U	S	O	M	E	G	J	Z	K	L	T	E
I	D	T	A	L	B	R	A	I	N	W	A	S	H	E	C	N
I	N	T	R	W	L	G	S	B	T	B	O	G	C	T	I	E
I	E	H	U	E	N	I	I	T	E	A	Q	P	T	S	T	Z
S	Z	C	C	A	M	L	R	N	K	E	N	R	D	I	S	L
R	W	G	T	T	L	I	K	E	N	C	I	O	P	J	E	K
L	M	E	V	E	Y	F	S	E	U	A	O	S	D	P	M	K
G	N	I	D	N	U	O	W	T	L	G	E	N	E	Z	O	D
Z	S	L	A	C	I	D	A	R	S	D	C	U	K	J	D	Y

Within two months, she was caught on video helping to rob a bank. The FBI launched a massive search to find her and to quash the SLA, eventually arresting Hearst in San Francisco. Although she served two years in prison, President Carter commuted her sentence and she was later pardoned.

Answers on page 190.

The Spy of Pearl Harbor

AIRCRAFT	DORMER	PROOF
ATTACK	FATEFUL	SAIL
BED	FINGERS	SENTENCED
BOAT	FOUND	SHEETS
CARRIERS	GUILTY	SIGNALS
CLOTHES	HEADLIGHTS	SPYING
CODED	LABOR	STAR
COMPLEX	LEADING	TRAGIC
CONSULATE	LINEN	WATERS
DAYS	MOVEMENTS	WINDOWS
DEPORTED	NATIONAL	

When the Japanese attacked Pearl Harbor on the Hawaiian island of Oahu on December 7, 1941, they had help from someone living on the island. A month earlier, a German citizen named Bernard Julius Otto Kuehn had offered to sell details about U.S. warships to the Japanese consulate in Hawaii.

D	I	T	L	R	E	M	R	O	D	R	O	B	A	L	Q	L
S	F	E	B	S	S	E	H	T	O	L	C	H	R	D	H	S
E	I	O	S	I	T	L	O	U	D	E	P	O	R	T	E	D
N	A	Y	R	W	F	E	K	C	A	T	T	A	J	M	H	O
T	S	E	E	B	I	H	E	A	D	L	I	G	H	T	S	Z
E	R	W	I	E	Q	N	N	H	A	S	P	Y	I	N	G	M
N	E	A	R	D	M	R	D	I	S	Y	G	G	Y	U	E	E
C	G	T	R	C	J	O	R	O	L	A	N	O	I	T	A	N
E	N	E	A	K	U	C	V	F	W	E	I	C	O	D	E	D
D	I	R	C	G	R	R	D	E	T	S	P	R	O	O	F	F
T	F	S	Z	A	W	L	A	A	M	L	V	L	M	D	X	A
R	R	Y	F	L	G	C	L	T	U	E	I	G	N	N	E	T
A	T	T	K	U	P	U	U	L	S	A	N	G	N	U	L	E
G	S	X	I	I	S	J	T	I	S	D	W	T	Z	O	P	F
I	S	L	A	N	G	I	S	N	N	I	K	T	S	F	M	U
C	T	M	O	J	K	J	D	E	K	N	M	N	C	O	O	L
Y	D	C	B	C	C	O	J	N	K	G	S	Y	A	D	C	E

Although the FBI had been suspicious of Kuehn for years, they never had proof of any wrongdoing until after the Pearl Harbor attack. When agents showed up at the Japanese consulate, they were able to stop officials from burning documents that implicated Kuehn. Kuehn was sentenced to 50 years of hard labor, and was later deported.

 Answers on page 190.

The Pizza Connection

BANISHED	FREQUENTLY	PARLORS
BRUTALLY	FRICTION	PIZZA
BUSINESS	GODFATHER	PROFITS
CARTELS	INFORMATION	PROLIFIC
CONDUCTED	LUCRATIVE	QUICKLY
CREW	MAFIA	RETALIATION
CUSTODY	MEDIA	RIVAL
DRAGNET	MOBSTERS	SICILIAN
DRUG	NEXUS	TROVE
FLIGHT	OPERATIVE	WARRANTS
FORMER	PARAPHERNALIA	

In 1985, the longest criminal jury trial in U.S. history began. Over 16 months, the FBI offered evidence of a drug cartel that spanned the globe, from Asia to America. After the leader of the cartel, Gaetano Badalamenti, was arrested in Madrid, he led the FBI to more than 20 other Sicilians who had been working for him in the U.S.

X	A	I	F	A	M	N	N	K	C	F	S	C	R	E	W	G
M	J	F	P	B	S	F	O	T	O	P	T	O	E	H	U	U
O	J	E	H	R	C	R	I	L	N	T	N	C	T	C	R	R
B	E	J	B	U	A	I	T	U	D	H	A	I	A	X	Y	D
S	V	P	A	T	R	C	A	C	U	G	R	F	L	P	L	M
T	I	R	N	A	T	T	M	R	C	I	R	I	I	N	K	P
E	T	O	I	L	E	I	R	A	T	L	A	L	A	E	C	I
R	A	F	S	L	L	O	O	T	E	F	W	O	T	X	I	Z
S	R	I	H	Y	S	N	F	I	D	H	B	R	I	U	U	Z
A	E	T	E	I	A	W	N	V	U	O	N	P	O	S	Q	A
S	P	S	D	I	M	W	I	E	D	R	A	G	N	E	T	C
R	O	Z	D	P	A	R	A	P	H	E	R	N	A	L	I	A
O	G	E	S	Z	H	I	G	O	D	F	A	T	H	E	R	F
L	M	A	R	I	V	A	L	Y	D	O	T	S	U	C	Y	H
R	R	R	S	S	E	N	I	S	U	B	A	T	R	O	V	E
A	S	I	C	I	L	I	A	N	R	E	M	R	O	F	J	G
P	Q	S	Y	L	T	N	E	U	Q	E	R	F	L	D	W	P

The cartel would buy morphine in Turkey, process it into heroin in Sicily, then smuggle it to the U.S., where it was often sold through innocuous-looking pizza shops. The media called the case "The Pizza Connection," and when it was all over, 18 men had been convicted, including Badalamenti.

 Answers on page 191.

Nussbaum and Wilcoxson

ALIASES	ELECTRONICS	MASSIVE
ARSENAL	ENEMIES	NAMES
AWRY	ENTREPRENEUR	OFFBEAT
BANK	ESTRANGED	PLED
BARELY	FIREARMS	REALIZED
BARREL	FUGITIVE	ROBBERS
BITTER	GANGSTER	SHOELACE
CACHE	HEATED	SHOTGUN
CAPITAL	HIDDEN	WEAPONS
COUNTRYSIDE	HOMEMADE	YEARS
DISGUISES	KNOCK	

Albert Nussbaum and Bobby Wilcoxson met in prison, but neither was reformed by the experience. After they were released, the two partnered up and successfully robbed eight banks before they were finally caught. Their downfall came after adding a new man named Peter Curry to their crew.

E	S	T	R	A	N	G	E	D	A	M	E	M	O	H	U	L
Y	C	O	U	N	T	R	Y	S	I	D	E	J	O	G	X	Y
W	S	H	R	U	E	N	E	R	P	E	R	T	N	E	V	Y
Q	N	S	H	O	T	G	U	N	L	S	E	S	A	I	L	A
D	O	S	H	L	J	M	M	E	A	F	C	J	R	C	R	B
I	P	E	Q	X	U	P	R	R	U	I	A	N	E	F	E	A
S	A	I	H	D	K	R	S	G	N	F	L	E	A	S	T	N
G	E	M	E	V	A	E	I	O	I	O	E	D	L	M	T	K
U	W	E	J	B	N	T	R	B	O	J	O	D	I	R	I	S
I	H	N	C	A	I	T	M	E	A	T	H	I	Z	A	B	R
S	E	E	L	V	C	P	S	A	H	R	S	H	E	E	T	E
E	A	I	E	E	M	L	E	W	S	C	E	F	D	R	Y	B
S	T	W	L	T	B	E	M	I	K	S	A	L	V	I	E	B
S	E	E	O	S	N	D	A	I	N	J	I	C	Y	F	A	O
X	D	A	W	R	Y	X	N	M	O	I	I	V	J	T	R	R
O	F	F	B	E	A	T	H	C	C	D	Q	S	E	C	S	P
N	G	A	N	G	S	T	E	R	K	L	A	T	I	P	A	C

The trio attempted to rob a bank in Brooklyn, but a botched plan resulted in a murdered guard and witnesses who contacted the police. The three fugitives went into hiding, but Curry was quickly arrested and told the FBI everything he knew about the other men. They were each apprehended soon after and sentenced to life in prison.

 Answers on page 191.

Timothy McVeigh

AREA	HISTORY	RESCUE
ATTACK	HOMEGROWN	SECURITY
BODY	IGNITED	SHOP
CARS	JAIL	SOLDIER
COMMIT	LOCKED	TROOPER
DEVASTATING	MINUTES	TWISTED
DOORS	MISSING	VEHICLE
DOZENS	MORNING	WAR
EXPLODED	OBSERVANT	WORST
GETAWAY	PANCAKES	ZONE
GUARD	POWERFUL	

When a bomb exploded outside the Alfred P. Murrah Federal Building in Oklahoma City on April 19, 1995, it was the worst act of domestic terrorism the country had ever seen. The bomb, which killed 168 people, had been fashioned from fertilizer and chemicals packed into a Ryder rental truck.

R	E	I	D	L	O	S	W	V	E	H	I	C	L	E	H	Z
G	D	H	L	D	T	L	O	C	K	E	D	L	G	O	D	P
U	S	H	O	P	R	D	E	T	I	N	G	I	N	T	O	A
A	B	O	D	Y	E	X	P	L	O	D	E	D	I	T	Z	N
R	D	O	B	S	E	R	V	A	N	T	H	M	S	B	E	C
D	P	B	A	Z	R	A	J	N	M	N	I	Q	S	T	N	A
R	T	O	G	R	O	O	Z	G	I	A	S	E	I	F	S	K
V	G	T	W	N	E	N	O	G	N	T	T	Y	M	Z	H	E
T	N	D	Y	E	I	A	E	D	U	T	O	D	B	O	L	S
I	I	E	T	R	R	T	T	R	T	A	R	C	M	R	T	N
M	N	U	I	O	E	F	A	M	E	C	Y	E	R	E	W	F
M	R	C	R	L	S	P	U	T	S	K	G	J	R	X	I	E
O	O	S	U	J	R	X	O	L	S	R	T	A	K	L	S	E
C	M	E	C	P	A	I	G	O	O	A	W	S	I	J	T	U
B	G	R	E	Y	C	O	Q	W	R	R	V	A	R	O	E	T
V	Z	H	S	P	D	H	N	R	H	T	J	E	A	O	D	X
I	F	P	Y	A	W	A	T	E	G	I	T	V	D	Z	W	R

The FBI quickly found the truck's axle in the rubble and used the vehicle identification number to trace it to a body shop. After interviewing employees, they had a name: Tim McVeigh. The FBI amassed over three tons of evidence against the bomber and two accomplices, and the three men were quickly convicted.

Answers on page 191.

Operation Greylord

ABUSE	HELP	POLITIC
ANNALS	IMPORTANT	PRIORITY
AUTHORITY	INTEGRITY	PUBLIC
BRIBES	INTENSE	STING
CLEANING	JUDGES	STRIKE
CORRUPTION	LOCAL	SYSTEMIC
COURTROOM	MAJOR	TABLE
CREDIBILITY	MAMMOTH	TICKETS
CROOKED	OFFICIALS	TRUST
CURLY	ORDER	WIGS
GUILTY	PLEADING	

In 1984, the FBI launched a massive sting operation in Cook County, Illinois. Named Operation Greylord in honor of the wigs worn by British judges, the agency worked with local judges and lawyers who posed as unethical officials in order to weed out actual corruption. The first to be found guilty was traffic court clerk Harold Conn, who had accepted bribes in exchange for fixing tickets.

C	L	E	A	N	I	N	G	S	C	I	B	T	A	B	L	E
A	U	T	H	O	R	I	T	Y	P	T	Y	C	T	C	C	P
D	H	P	G	S	E	B	I	R	B	H	I	N	U	O	R	O
W	W	G	G	F	G	I	I	N	C	M	A	R	R	O	J	L
W	I	N	U	H	N	O	N	I	E	T	L	R	J	U	X	I
G	G	I	I	Q	R	F	N	T	R	Y	U	A	D	P	C	T
N	S	T	L	I	B	T	S	O	E	P	M	G	V	U	W	I
I	M	S	T	Y	E	Y	P	X	T	G	E	D	X	B	M	C
D	O	Y	Y	N	S	M	M	I	V	S	R	E	O	L	O	F
A	F	P	S	M	I	J	O	K	M	R	Y	I	L	I	O	E
E	F	E	J	C	K	N	L	O	C	A	L	M	T	C	R	K
L	I	F	Y	T	I	L	I	B	I	D	E	R	C	Y	T	I
P	C	W	D	E	K	O	O	R	C	R	F	A	R	P	R	R
Y	I	D	H	P	G	N	M	P	T	S	U	R	T	Z	U	T
M	A	E	O	R	D	E	R	A	N	N	A	L	S	O	O	S
I	L	S	T	E	K	C	I	T	E	S	U	B	A	O	C	A
P	S	Q	E	C	J	Z	N	Z	H	T	O	M	M	A	M	X

From there, the indictments kept rolling in, until 92 officials, including judges, lawyers, police officers, and a state legislator, had been arrested. The operation shined a light on the importance of ending public corruption.

 Answers on page 191.

Fraud in the Defense Department

ABUSE	GOVERNING	PROPRIETARY
BID	HONEST	PROVERB
BRIBES	INFORMATION	SCANDAL
CONSULTANT	LATER	SECRETARY
CONTRACTORS	LUCRATIVE	SIGNIFICANT
CRIMES	MANY	SYSTEMS
DETERMINE	MOUNTAIN	TOOL
ELECTRONIC	OFFICIALS	WARRANTS
ENABLED	PARTNERS	WEAPONS
ENGLISH	PENTAGON	WIRETAP
FRAUD	PROCUREMENT	

In 1986, a military consultant in Virginia offered a defense contractor proprietary bid information from a competitor in exchange for cash. But instead of taking the consultant up on the offer, the contractor relayed the conversation to the FBI. As they looked into the case, the FBI realized they had enough evidence to investigate with surveillance and wiretaps, in an undertaking codenamed Operation Illwind.

D	S	C	O	N	O	F	F	I	C	I	A	L	S	G	F	D
S	E	M	R	P	X	B	R	E	V	O	R	P	N	T	I	A
E	C	L	T	I	A	F	S	T	O	O	L	O	C	B	B	Y
B	R	W	B	N	M	R	A	M	S	C	I	L	S	U	L	R
I	E	N	E	A	E	E	T	T	E	T	B	W	S	C	C	A
R	T	G	D	L	N	M	S	N	A	T	N	E	O	P	O	T
B	A	J	O	Q	E	E	E	M	E	I	S	N	Y	E	N	E
E	R	S	O	V	N	C	R	R	A	R	T	Y	I	N	S	I
N	Y	C	Z	O	E	O	T	T	U	R	S	W	S	T	U	R
I	H	A	H	S	F	R	N	R	A	C	W	Y	D	A	L	P
M	S	N	C	N	T	U	N	C	O	I	O	U	J	G	T	O
R	I	D	I	G	O	N	T	I	R	N	A	R	G	O	A	R
E	L	A	M	M	M	O	A	E	N	R	I	N	P	N	N	P
T	G	L	A	R	R	T	T	R	F	G	I	C	S	P	T	V
E	N	R	N	S	L	A	T	E	R	W	E	A	P	O	N	S
D	E	R	Y	D	P	E	V	I	T	A	R	C	U	L	K	D
T	N	A	C	I	F	I	N	G	I	S	W	Q	M	L	X	Y

The operation uncovered a string of defense procurement fraud that resulted in the prosecution of more than 60 officials. It also led to new rules governing federal procurement, spelled out in the Procurement Integrity Act.

 Answers on page 192.

Pine Ridge Murders

AGENT
ALLEGE
CONTINGENT
EVIDENCE
EXAMINATION
EXTRACTED
FACTS
FIRE
FOOT
INDICATED
LABORATORY
MATCH
MEMBERS
MURDERED
OCCUPANTS
OPERABLE
OPINIONS
OUTSTANDING
PRESENT
PREVIOUS
PROSECUTION
RADIO
RIFLE
ROUNDS
SHELL
SMOOTH
TOTAL
TRANSMISSION
TURNPIKE
UNKNOWN
VEHICLE
WARRANT

The remote location of the Pine Ridge Indian Reservation in southwest South Dakota may explain why Leonard Peltier, a fugitive who was wanted for the attempted murder of a police officer, was on the reservation on June 26, 1975. On the same day, two FBI agents, Jack Coler and Ronald Williams, encountered Peltier, who assumed the agents were there to arrest him.

T	U	R	N	P	I	K	E	J	P	Q	Z	F	A	A	N	R
Z	M	L	N	P	G	T	N	R	S	A	O	Q	L	O	T	A
S	Z	U	F	O	O	I	E	B	S	O	D	L	I	N	F	D
T	T	B	R	T	I	S	S	D	T	E	E	T	E	B	A	I
N	L	R	A	D	E	T	N	R	T	G	U	G	B	G	C	O
A	L	L	A	N	E	U	A	C	E	C	A	S	L	N	T	N
P	A	N	T	N	O	R	A	N	E	B	G	V	X	I	S	S
U	B	I	D	R	S	R	E	S	I	E	M	W	U	D	O	N
C	O	V	T	E	T	M	O	D	V	M	A	E	N	N	P	O
C	R	L	E	X	T	R	I	I	B	R	A	W	M	A	E	I
O	A	L	E	H	P	A	D	S	R	B	O	X	E	T	R	N
M	T	E	V	W	I	E	C	A	S	N	S	R	E	S	A	I
M	O	H	G	Q	N	C	N	I	K	I	I	M	O	T	B	P
A	R	S	L	C	I	T	L	N	D	F	O	E	O	U	L	O
T	Y	Y	E	Q	B	J	U	E	Q	N	P	N	J	O	E	D
C	K	S	U	O	I	V	E	R	P	R	I	F	L	E	T	O
H	W	B	H	W	N	T	N	E	G	N	I	T	N	O	C	H

He fired at their cars with an AR-15 rifle, killing both men, who, ironically, were on the reservation to arrest someone else. It didn't take long for the FBI to match shell casings to Peltier's rifle, and he was sentenced to two life terms in prison.

 Answers on page 192.

The UAF 855 Hijacking

AIRCRAFT	FLIGHT	PARACHUTES
ALTIMETER	FOURTEEN	PISTOL
ASSESS	FURNISHED	SHERIFF
BOARDED	GRENADE	SKIES
CAPTAIN	GUNMAN	STEEL
COCKPIT	HIJACK	STEWARDESS
COURIER	IMPRESSION	STOPOVER
CULVERT	NEARBY	STUMBLED
DETONATE	OBJECT	SURPRISING
DISCREETLY	OBSERVED	TAKEOFF
ENVELOPE	PACK	

Richard Floyd McCoy Jr. was a Vietnam veteran, helicopter pilot, and experienced skydiver who had fallen into hard financial times. So on April 7, 1972, he took drastic measures: he hijacked a Los Angeles-bound plane. McCoy produced a hand grenade and gun and demanded the pilot divert to San Francisco, where he asked for $500,000 and four parachutes.

G M T Q D F L I G H T L O T S I P
S N R C J E Y I M P R E S S I O N
P E Y C U K D S U R P R I S I N G
A A D N C L C R N D E L B M U T S
R R B A B O V E A T F F I R E H S
A B P R C A E E E O N I A T P A C
C Y Y K X T I M R A B X S K I E S
H B P L R T I R M T T A K E O F F
U I R U T T S N C T L G H B K T I
T W O E L E U G B R H F Y S C C E
E F P A V G E B R M A T J S A E T
S X C U C O U R I E R F H E J J A
L U P D T L P Y C I N W T S I B N
I N L E E T S O D S C A R S H O O
S S E D R A W E T S I H D A I J T
D E H S I N R U F S B D V E E G E
K E P O L E V N E O B S E R V E D

After releasing the passengers, McCoy told the pilot to fly over Utah, where he bailed out of the plane. The FBI was able to find McCoy's fingerprints on the plane, and witnesses in Provo, Utah, saw him on the ground directly after the hijacking. He was arrested and sentenced to 45 years in prison.

Answers on page 192.

An FBI Betrayal

AFFIDAVIT	DAMAGE	METHODS
ARRESTED	DEVOTED	MISSION
ATTORNEY	DISKETTES	NUMEROUS
BEGIN	DIVISION	OUTSTANDING
CAREER	DROP	PACKAGE
CHARGED	EARN	PAROLE
CLASSIFIED	EVIDENCE	PENETRATION
CLEAR	FULL	PRIVATE
COMMIT	GOVERNED	PUNISHED
CONGRESS	GRATITUDE	QUIETLY
CONSPIRACY	GRAVE	

As far back as 1985, FBI Counterintelligence Agent Robert Hanssen had been passing along classified information to Russia and the former Soviet Union. The veteran agent was finally caught in 2001, after his own colleagues began an investigation into his actions and discovered a Russian document naming him as an American spy.

V	G	O	V	E	R	N	E	D	H	L	L	U	F	G	T	N
N	O	I	S	S	I	M	C	A	R	E	E	R	E	Y	R	R
T	W	D	I	V	I	S	I	O	N	M	N	M	G	D	C	A
P	I	M	Y	D	L	S	S	E	R	G	N	O	C	E	J	E
A	C	M	E	L	A	Y	E	N	R	O	T	T	A	T	C	Q
C	D	H	M	T	T	M	H	T	D	T	G	R	N	O	O	N
K	E	E	A	O	H	E	A	E	Y	I	R	A	O	V	N	U
A	D	C	H	R	C	O	I	G	N	V	A	E	I	E	S	M
G	O	E	N	S	G	F	D	U	E	A	T	L	T	D	P	E
E	T	G	T	E	I	E	A	S	Q	D	I	C	A	T	I	R
G	L	Z	D	S	D	N	D	J	G	I	T	D	R	Q	R	O
T	R	O	S	R	E	I	U	P	I	F	U	Z	T	B	A	U
K	S	A	R	D	O	R	V	P	W	F	D	G	E	S	C	S
M	L	C	V	A	V	P	R	E	Y	A	E	G	N	W	Y	S
C	X	L	H	E	P	C	N	A	V	O	I	C	E	D	Z	V
E	O	U	T	S	T	A	N	D	I	N	G	V	P	X	E	L
S	E	T	T	E	K	S	I	D	P	R	I	V	A	T	E	F

Hanssen, who worked in key counterintelligence positions, had managed to pass along more than 6,000 pages of material to the Russians, in exchange for diamonds and cash. Considered the most damaging spy in FBI history, Hanssen pled guilty to espionage and was sentenced to life in prison.

 Answers on page 192.

Answer Key

Notorious
(page 4)

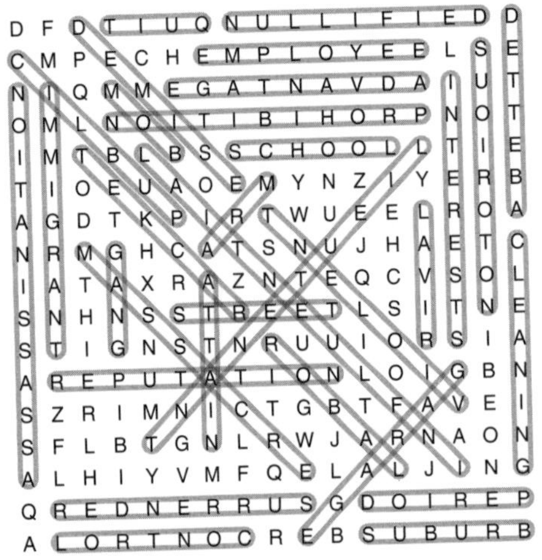

The Martin Durkin Manhunt (page 8)

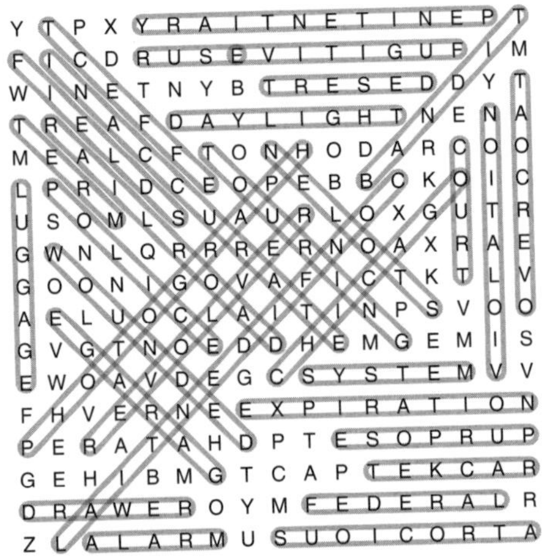

The Case of Ana Montes
(page 6)

The Amerithrax Investigation (page 10)

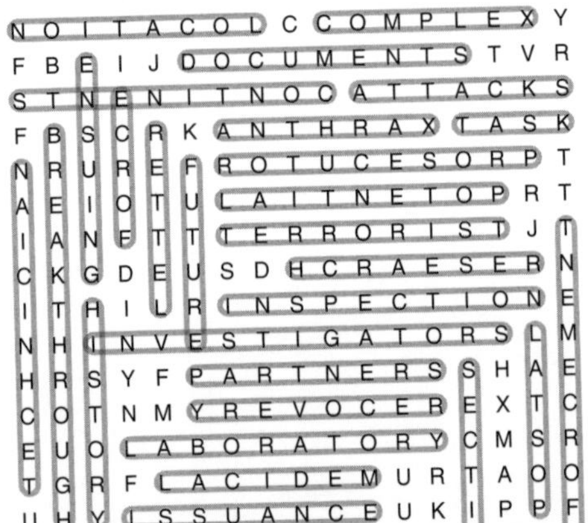

Answer Key

The Teflon Don
(page 12)

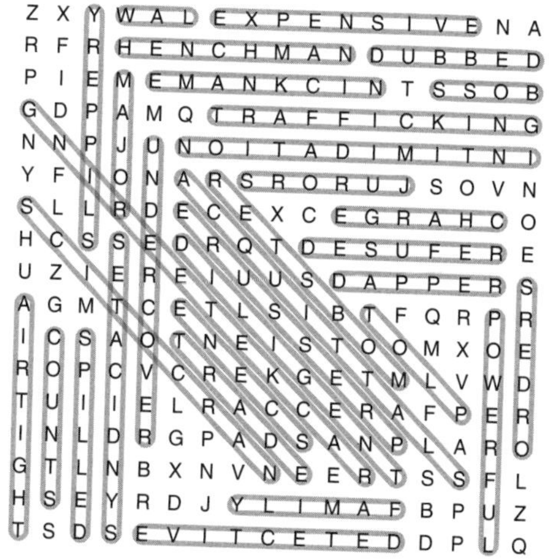

1996 Summer Olympics Bomber (page 16)

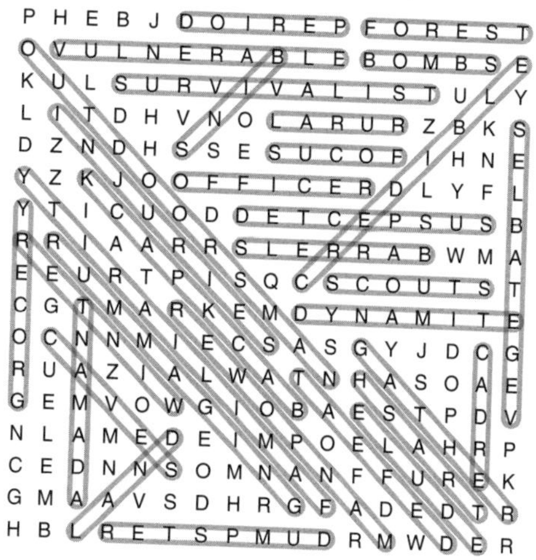

The Demise of Enron
(page 14)

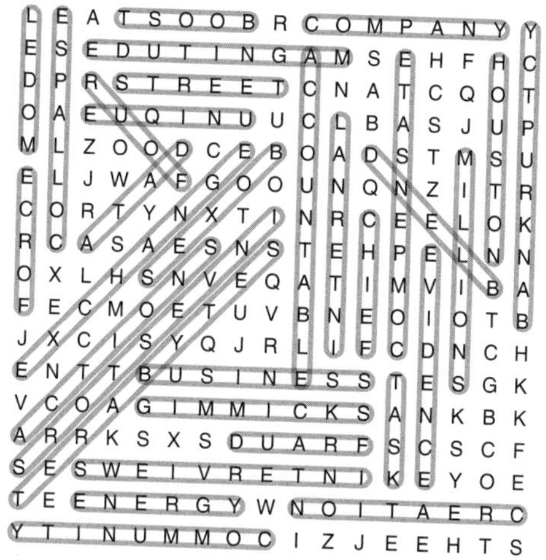

Marian Zacharski
(page 18)

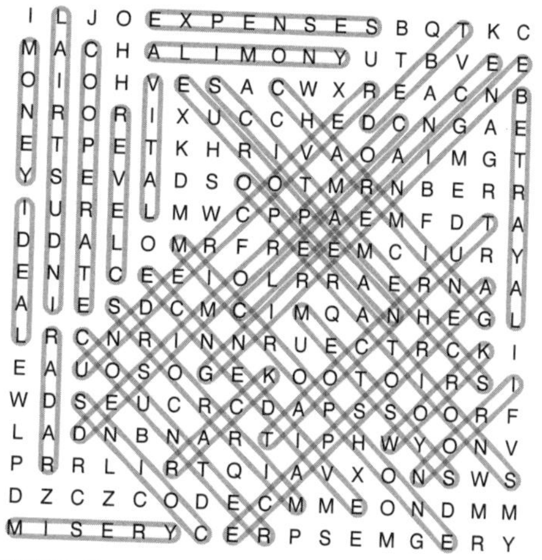

Answer Key

Operation Shrouded Horizon (page 20)

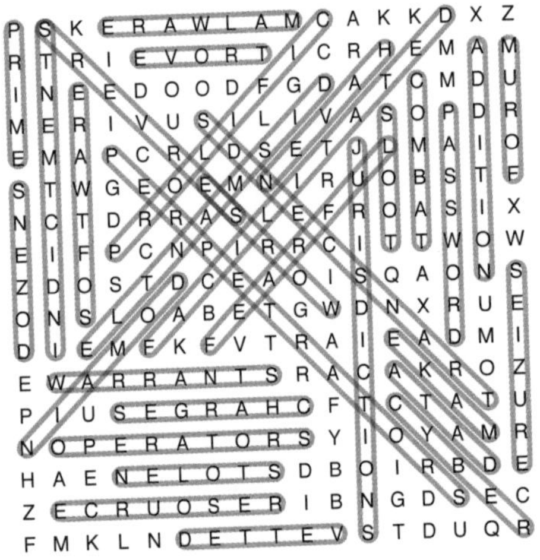

The Dixie Mafia Manhunt (page 24)

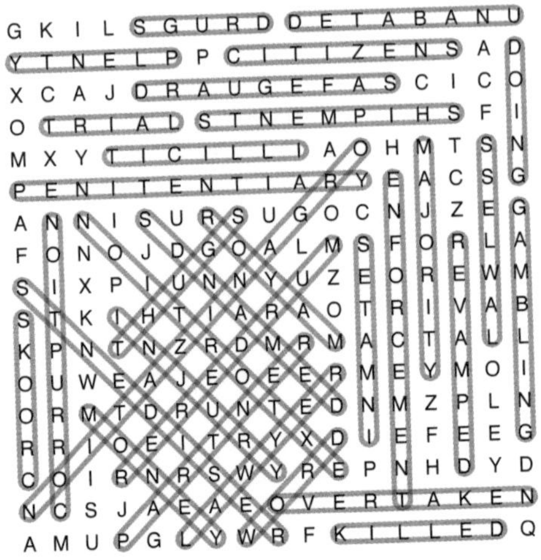

A $10 Million Hack (page 22)

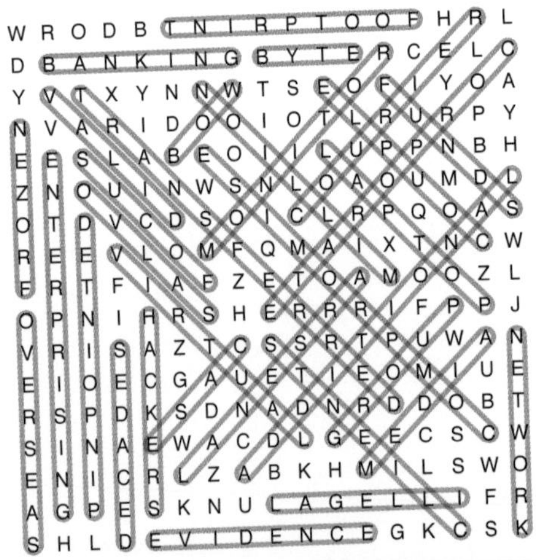

Sergey Viktorovich Petrov (page 26)

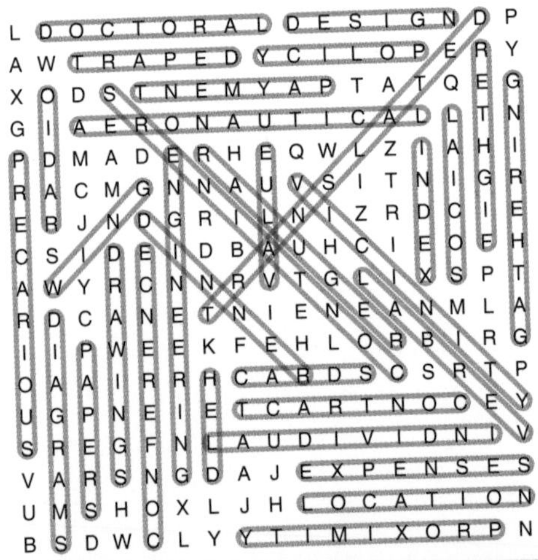

Answer Key

Testerman and Lovett
(page 28)

The Case of the Hollow Nickel (page 32)

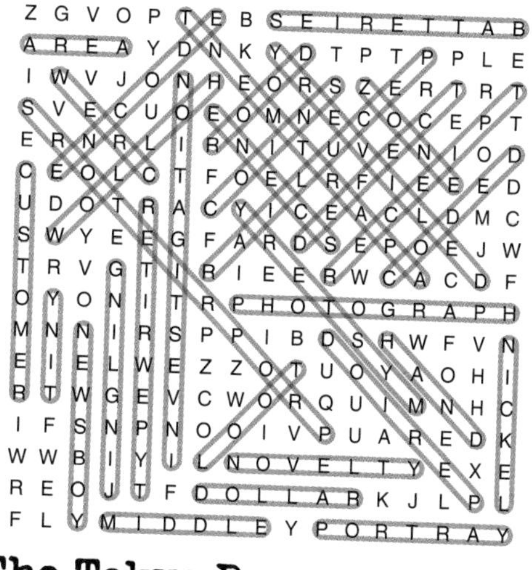

John Elgin Johnson
(page 30)

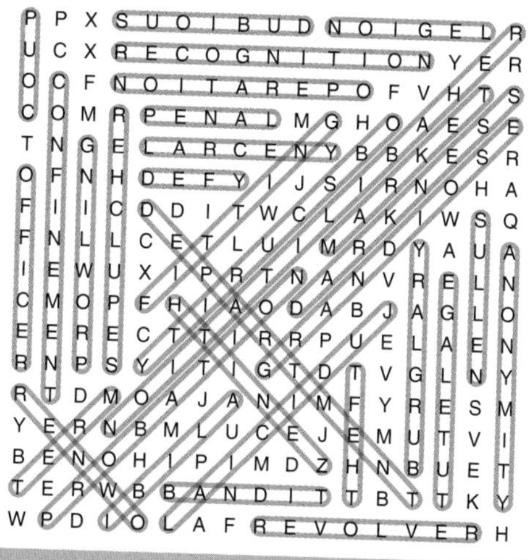

The Tokyo Rose
(page 34)

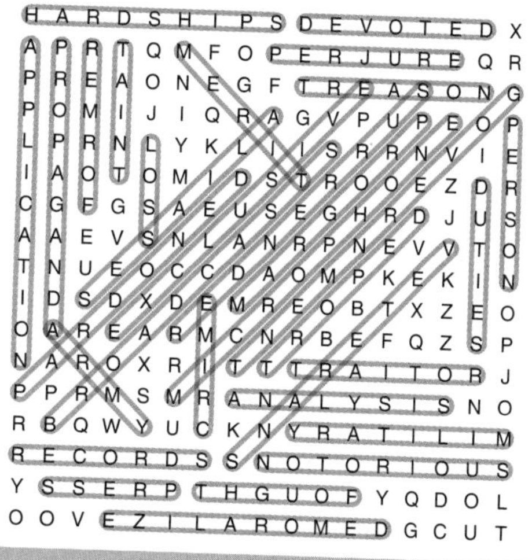

Answer Key

United Airlines Flight 629 (page 36)

The Melissa Virus (page 40)

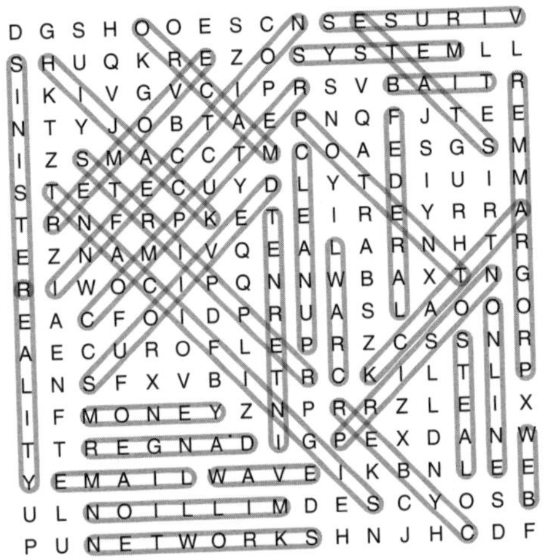

The Medgar Evers Assassination (page 38)

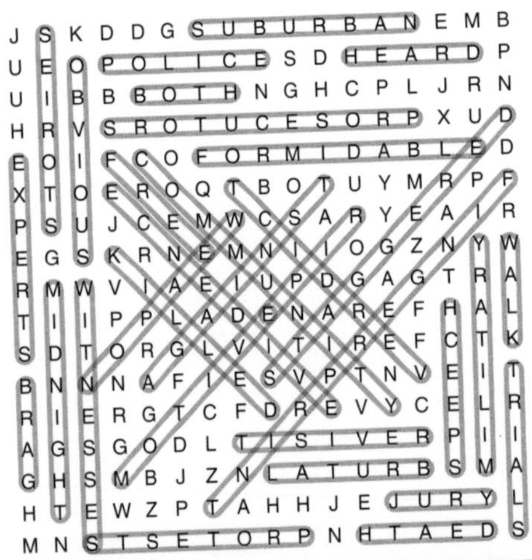

The Doll Woman (page 42)

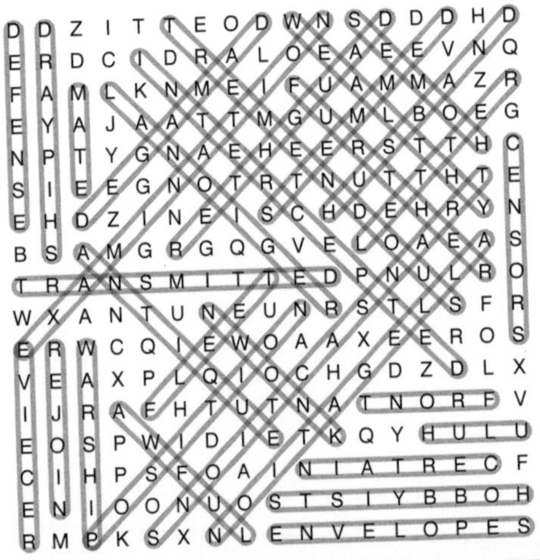

Answer Key

Vonsiatsky Espionage (page 44)

T	C	I	R	T	S	I	D	E	T	E	I	V	O	S	Q	A
N	X	M	A	J	O	R	L	R	R	E	S	U	L	T	T	M
O	R	W	R	L	B	P	V	U	S	M	L	D	G	T	J	Y
I	P	Y	O	C	R	A	N	T	T	P	O	E	E	A	T	F
T	S	C	I	G	O	S	F	C	C	C	R	N	A	I	N	G
U	T	A	N	E	T	S	E	U	K	A	D	I	R	D	N	N
C	E	R	E	R	H	A	I	R	J	W	S	A	E	I	E	B
E	L	I	S	M	E	G	H	T	Y	L	H	H	R	S	T	R
S	F	P	T	A	R	E	C	S	C	C	H	P	E	K	T	W
O	A	S	E	N	H	T	C	O	N	F	E	R	E	N	C	E
R	E	N	N	M	O	C	F	A	S	C	I	S	T	S	F	U
P	L	O	S	C	O	B	A	C	K	G	R	O	U	N	D	F
U	X	C	I	L	D	O	P	P	O	R	T	U	N	I	T	Y
Z	E	L	O	S	D	E	Z	I	L	A	R	U	T	A	N	V
Y	H	N	N	R	E	V	O	L	U	T	I	O	N	A	R	Y
N	E	Z	I	T	I	C	T	N	E	U	Q	E	S	B	U	S
L	S	U	M	M	E	R	F	I	C	T	I	T	I	O	U	S

ABSCAM (page 48)

E	D	S	Q	B	O	G	U	S	R	O	T	A	N	E	S	I
C	S	E	T	N	E	L	U	D	U	A	R	F	S	V	G	N
N	O	H	T	S	E	R	E	T	N	I	D	S	G	N	R	V
A	U	W	E	C	P	X	V	Q	B	O	E	N	I	G	E	E
T	V	E	X	I	I	A	S	T	Z	N	I	T	N	S	B	S
R	N	S	C	F	K	V	Q	E	I	K	E	I	N	S	D	T
O	O	A	S	A	J	F	N	S	C	V	T	E	O	D	E	I
P	I	C	G	E	K	J	U	O	I	S	C	O	K	R	L	G
M	T	E	N	N	Y	B	H	R	C	I	W	K	A	A	J	A
I	A	P	I	T	P	E	D	D	L	I	N	G	E	U	F	T
W	R	O	T	R	T	P	U	R	R	O	C	M	X	G	I	I
O	E	L	N	A	B	G	A	M	B	L	I	N	G	E	G	O
R	P	E	I	P	M	R	T	P	U	B	L	I	C	F	U	N
K	O	V	A	M	G	N	I	D	L	O	F	N	U	A	I	E
G	N	N	P	E	B	Z	W	B	U	N	F	G	S	S	L	M
W	B	E	K	N	S	U	M	T	E	D	Z	B	J	Q	T	E
P	O	L	I	T	I	C	I	A	N	S	D	U	S	T	Y	I

Wall Street Bombing 1920 (page 46)

O	V	E	R	N	I	G	H	T	C	R	U	C	I	A	L	R
F	G	N	I	T	N	I	R	P	T	R	A	C	H	K	T	L
D	A	N	A	R	C	H	I	S	T	Z	A	V	A	L	A	A
I	R	C	W	F	R	Q	L	U	N	C	H	F	I	N	M	B
L	E	C	I	L	O	P	T	O	L	L	T	B	O	F	S	R
I	I	Q	N	Y	L	X	X	V	E	E	R	I	Q	U	X	E
G	B	A	D	E	V	Y	M	X	R	A	T	S	C	W	C	C
E	E	H	O	R	S	E	P	M	R	N	S	C	Z	R	S	O
N	G	P	W	S	K	L	A	Y	E	I	U	U	O	E	A	L
T	W	A	S	U	O	T	F	T	V	M	E	W	H	C	V	L
L	A	B	N	S	H	O	N	A	B	A	D	L	Y	N	N	E
Y	G	R	I	R	M	I	G	E	T	L	O	L	O	E	A	C
E	O	O	E	E	A	U	D	T	B	T	D	P	M	D	C	T
A	N	H	N	J	E	C	W	Y	R	I	A	R	R	I	M	I
S	V	T	W	D	B	Y	Q	O	V	A	V	C	W	V	W	O
D	E	F	I	R	E	A	I	A	R	U	C	I	K	E	A	N
D	R	G	N	I	L	L	I	K	F	E	D	E	V	U	O	S

Escape from Alcatraz (page 50)

U	R	L	H	K	L	E	Z	A	R	T	A	C	L	A	W	L
T	C	I	R	T	S	B	H	T	D	V	N	X	Y	R	C	B
K	P	F	Q	N	A	U	L	S	H	C	T	P	R	O	C	L
Z	S	E	L	U	R	T	E	H	O	G	N	D	N	E	R	Y
J	F	V	D	D	O	V	Z	Q	L	U	U	V	I	V	A	I
I	E	O	S	C	I	F	I	C	A	P	I	A	D	I	L	R
T	S	B	O	T	Y	A	N	P	O	C	K	S	C	S	R	O
E	R	T	A	L	W	F	I	M	T	T	Y	W	O	N	E	N
M	M	L	T	A	D	R	O	S	A	T	O	C	L	E	A	N
S	E	Y	T	P	E	U	Y	R	U	X	I	H	G	T	D	M
R	P	E	T	H	M	K	M	R	B	N	I	M	P	N	Y	Y
U	R	R	G	I	R	E	E	M	M	I	H	M	W	I	D	L
O	D	U	I	U	R	T	T	A	I	G	D	G	U	L	R	E
M	O	T	B	S	S	U	T	T	U	E	Z	D	O	M	A	N
T	C	B	S	A	O	E	C	O	A	I	S	C	I	W	U	O
N	E	B	L	E	S	N	R	E	Z	S	N	N	F	N	G	L
R	P	P	F	U	V	D	R	R	S	P	L	A	C	E	G	W

Answer Key

Bank Heist in Indiana (page 52)

D	C	F	O	Z	D	H	U	W	D	K	E	D	A	N	S	E
I	U	S	H	C	R	O	T	E	T	C	V	I	E	I	E	L
M	S	S	E	C	C	A	L	Z	O	K	N	M	G	A	I	C
U	T	R	E	V	O	I	V	M	L	D	R	A	P	A	T	I
S	O	A	G	E	N	E	M	Y	I	E	P	A	L	D	E	H
M	D	L	F	Q	T	I	N	C	I	P	R	O	W	V	I	E
A	Y	Y	U	A	T	O	T	H	R	O	O	A	A	I	R	V
P	W	E	T	X	L	M	S	E	L	T	C	J	E	S	A	S
O	N	S	I	E	E	A	H	E	E	S	C	A	P	B	V	E
T	B	X	F	N	C	E	D	G	M	O	T	O	R	D	O	N
I	Y	A	T	A	N	A	C	T	I	V	I	T	Y	L	C	T
L	F	I	N	D	Z	K	Y	T	L	I	U	G	N	R	E	E
V	W	A	E	K	Y	T	I	N	I	C	I	V	I	I	G	N
L	F	D	Y	C	N	E	M	E	L	C	F	S	G	C	R	C
N	O	I	T	A	G	O	R	R	E	T	N	I	H	P	A	E
K	P	Y	N	E	C	R	A	L	C	B	O	Z	T	P	H	D
P	P	E	T	T	Y	M	V	C	O	N	V	I	C	T	C	Z

The Murder of Judge Vance (page 56)

D	Q	L	I	N	K	E	D	M	O	T	I	V	E	W	N	K
D	E	T	P	E	C	R	E	T	N	I	K	O	U	A	U	S
P	X	R	C	E	E	G	A	K	C	A	P	P	M	P	R	E
A	P	E	C	C	X	L	B	S	U	S	P	E	C	T	S	G
R	S	X	O	S	A	T	M	T	A	D	Z	A	R	S	M	R
C	R	P	U	Y	N	E	E	V	N	Y	Q	E	S	E	I	A
E	T	L	R	A	I	Z	U	N	L	R	S	G	T	G	T	H
L	R	O	T	D	M	I	F	A	S	E	E	F	C	D	C	C
N	A	D	H	I	U	B	N	L	N	I	S	T	A	U	I	E
Q	I	E	O	L	S	A	O	T	U	E	V	F	T	J	V	S
M	L	D	U	O	V	I	M	M	R	F	F	E	N	A	I	O
E	J	G	S	H	R	E	W	I	B	Z	E	J	O	V	P	L
T	C	U	E	A	N	H	A	L	W	T	R	T	C	X	M	I
S	X	L	N	T	L	L	A	U	T	H	O	R	I	Z	E	D
Y	M	E	E	S	T	N	E	V	E	Z	S	G	N	P	N	A
S	C	A	L	A	R	E	D	E	F	E	Y	M	B	F	S	F
S	H	U	R	T	R	T	K	L	A	N	O	S	R	E	P	A

Aldrich Ames (page 54)

E	O	J	R	I	N	T	E	L	L	I	G	E	N	C	E	S
G	E	W	M	N	T	N	A	U	S	R	U	P	P	D	S	N
A	S	P	Y	I	N	G	D	E	F	E	I	R	B	E	D	O
N	S	A	E	S	R	E	V	O	A	L	G	Z	I	G	O	I
O	R	B	S	H	T	N	O	M	S	D	U	R	T	X	F	T
I	A	R	R	E	S	T	E	D	S	O	M	L	A	Z	F	A
P	S	J	J	X	V	S	R	E	I	C	E	A	R	H	I	R
S	I	L	P	S	O	E	K	I	G	U	E	R	G	D	C	E
E	D	H	L	E	L	I	I	N	N	M	T	E	E	M	E	P
S	E	X	E	C	U	T	E	D	M	E	I	D	T	E	R	O
N	N	V	A	R	N	I	V	G	E	N	N	E	E	T	S	J
A	T	E	S	E	T	R	R	V	N	T	G	F	D	S	T	U
I	I	T	T	T	E	O	R	F	T	S	S	P	B	Y	R	S
S	T	E	Y	L	E	H	R	E	B	O	T	C	O	S	A	T
S	I	R	H	Y	R	T	X	K	S	T	N	E	G	A	V	I
U	E	A	T	T	O	U	D	I	P	L	O	M	A	T	E	C
R	S	N	O	I	T	A	R	E	C	R	A	C	N	I	L	E

Theft of the Krupp Diamond (page 58)

L	D	N	O	I	T	C	U	A	T	Z	H	K	A	P	N	S
E	V	I	T	I	G	U	F	F	C	C	I	M	L	L	O	V
F	B	A	R	O	N	E	S	S	O	T	Q	B	O	A	D	D
O	T	G	R	O	C	E	R	Z	D	R	A	L	V	E	N	A
R	R	Z	T	H	I	E	V	E	S	G	T	J	E	P	I	D
E	A	I	T	G	V	Y	G	Y	U	F	E	U	D	P	M	A
M	N	G	O	U	E	E	E	E	H	W	D	E	N	A	R	W
A	S	Z	T	I	L	V	T	N	E	T	I	Y	K	E	E	C
N	P	A	K	L	B	T	I	L	O	T	L	R	M	H	T	Y
T	O	G	A	T	E	L	E	T	H	M	O	A	X	W	S	R
K	R	A	P	Y	X	R	O	E	C	W	C	X	E	G	A	T
R	T	K	L	P	B	F	R	O	E	A	R	R	A	W	M	N
A	E	R	W	J	L	T	K	M	D	Q	R	I	L	U	R	U
Z	D	N	J	D	A	F	O	R	C	E	D	T	N	A	O	O
K	E	V	N	O	M	H	K	P	S	W	R	S	T	G	M	C
E	O	M	V	I	E	K	M	H	C	N	A	R	O	A	U	T
R	Z	A	R	B	D	G	N	I	L	W	A	R	P	S	R	H

Answer Key

MIBURN
(page 60)

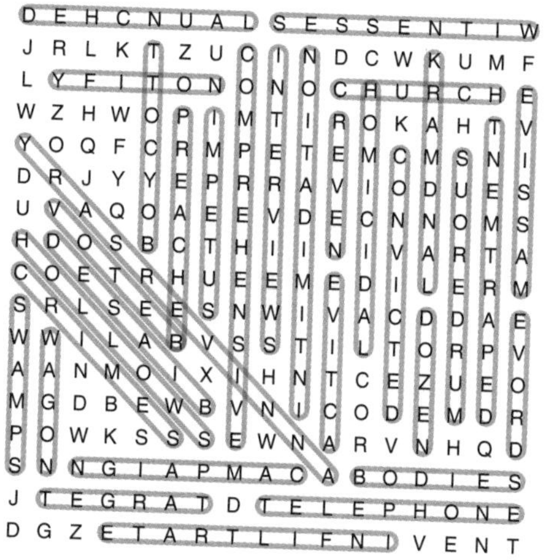

The 1993 WTC Bombing
(page 64)

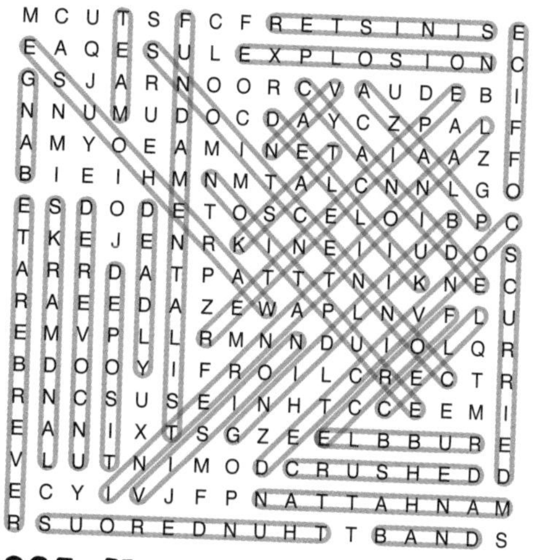

Congressman Jefferson
(page 62)

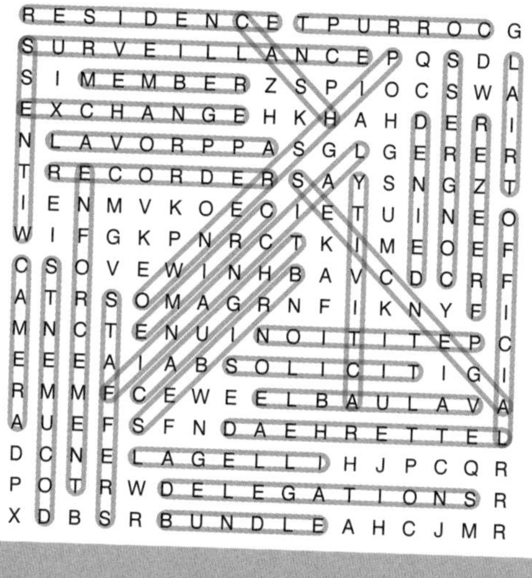

1985: Year of the Spy
(page 66)

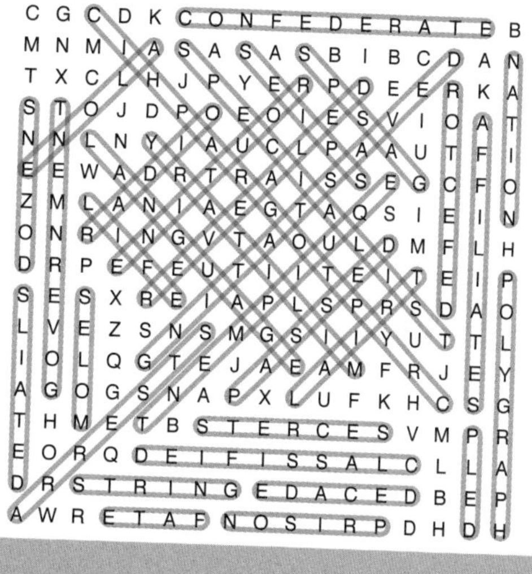

Answer Key

Alger Hiss
(page 68)

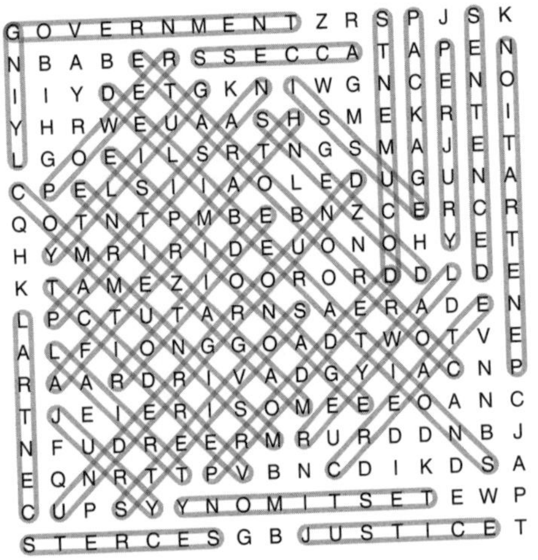

The Watergate Saga
(page 72)

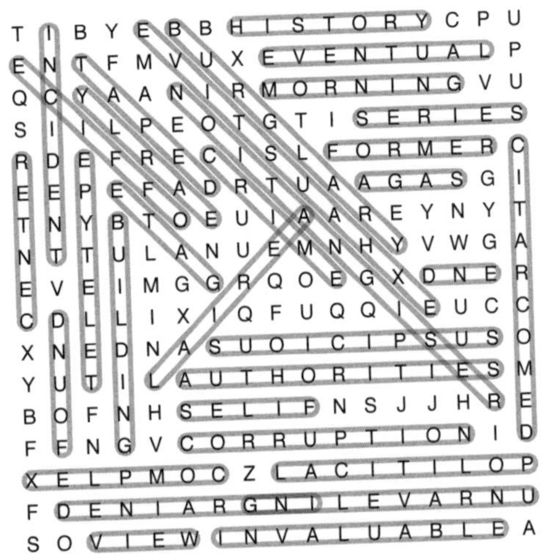

The Rosenbergs
(page 70)

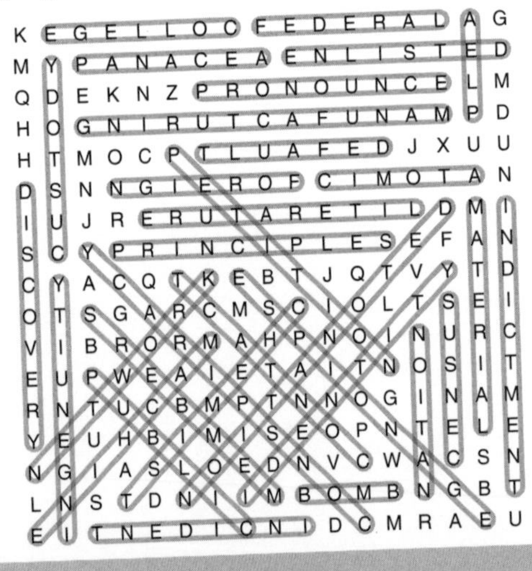

Weather Underground Bombings (page 74)

Answer Key

The Sixteenth Street Baptist Church (page 76)

Snipers on the Beltway (page 80)

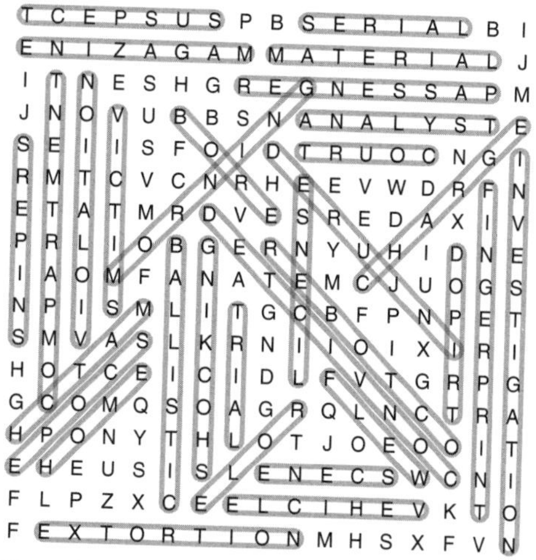

The Barker and Karpis Gang (page 78)

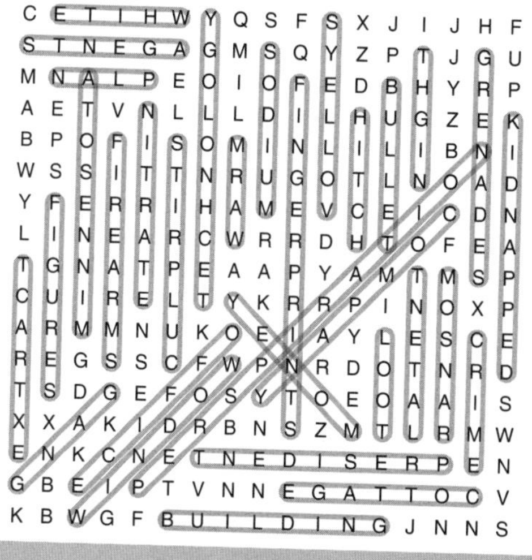

The Black Tom Railroad Yard Bombing (page 82)

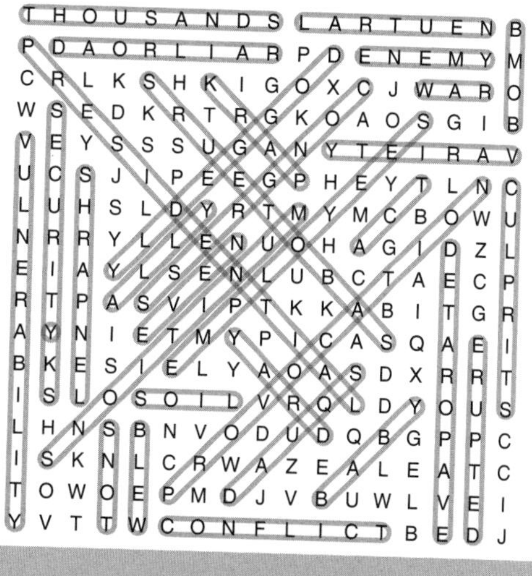

Answer Key

Brian P. Regan Espionage (page 84)

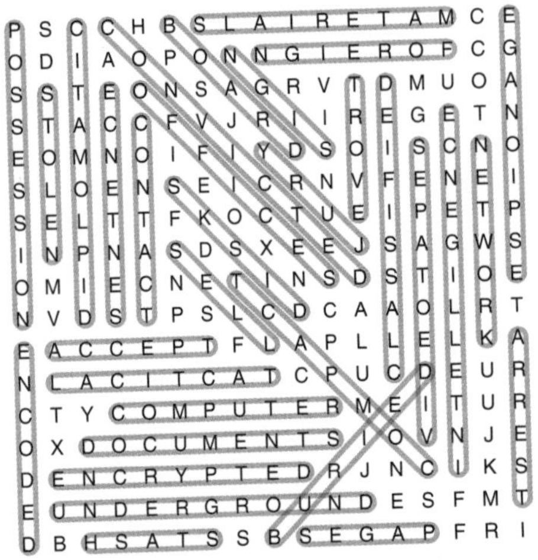

Child Kidnappers Go to Jail (page 88)

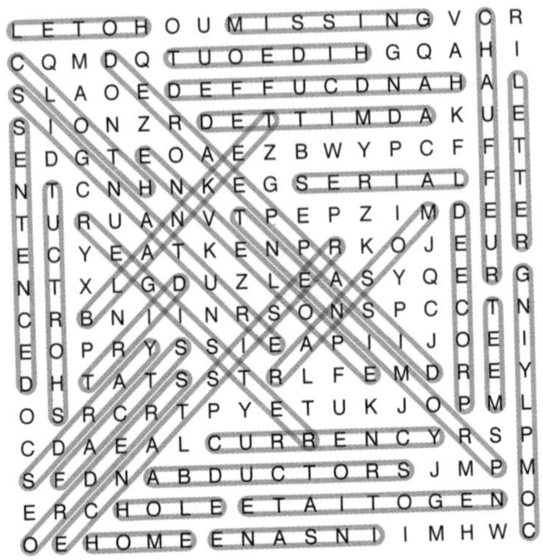

Weinberger Kidnapping (page 86)

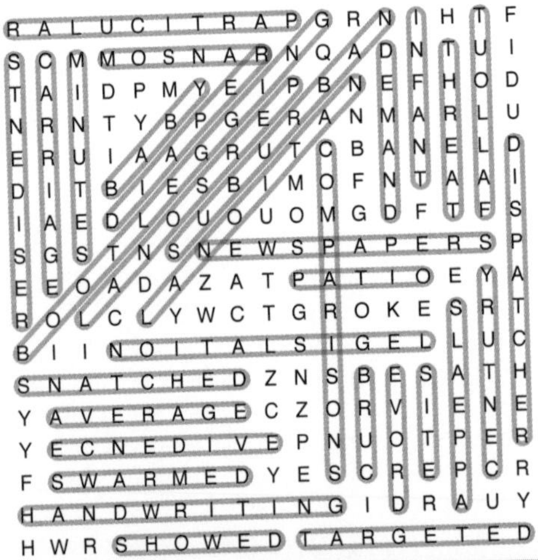

The Brink's Building Robbery (page 90)

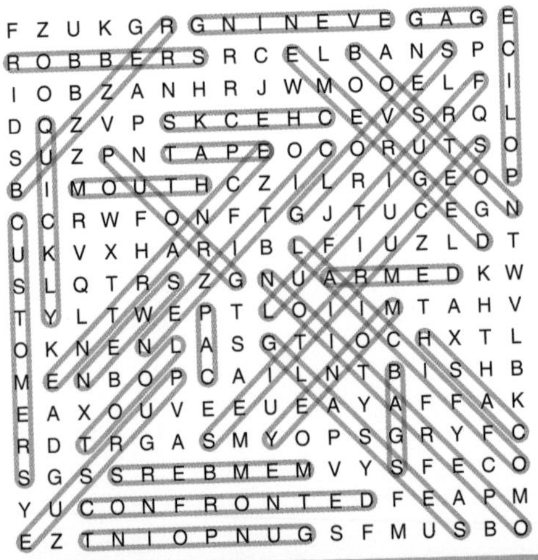

Answer Key

The Charles Ross Kidnapping (page 92)

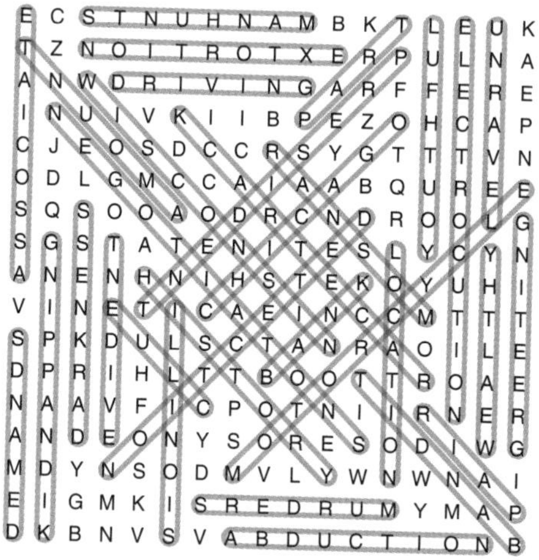

Soviet Espionage in the 1970s (page 96)

Fritz Duquesne, Nazi Spy (page 94)

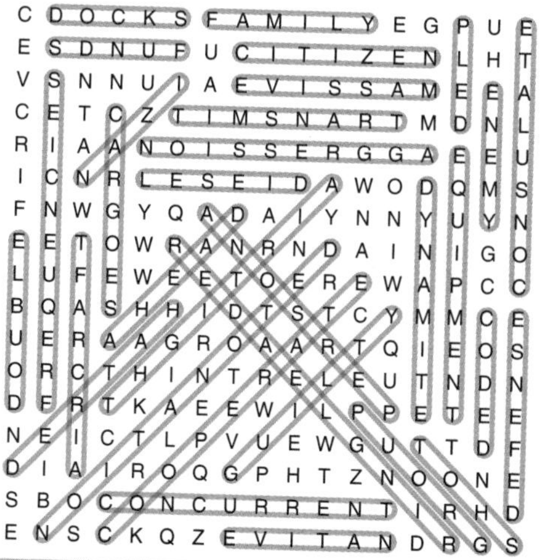

Telemarketing Fraud (page 98)

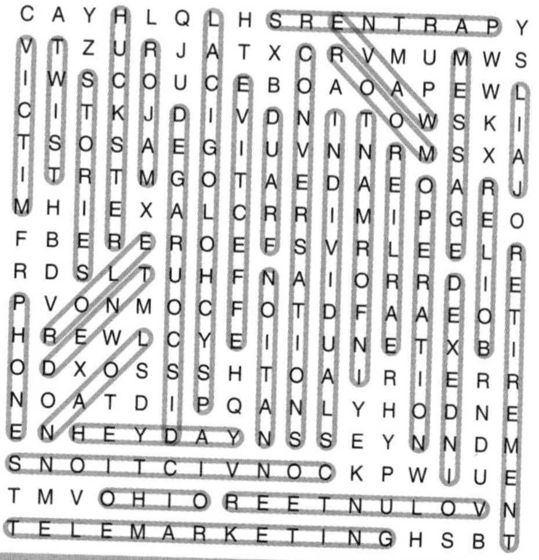

Answer Key

A WWII Double Agent (page 100)

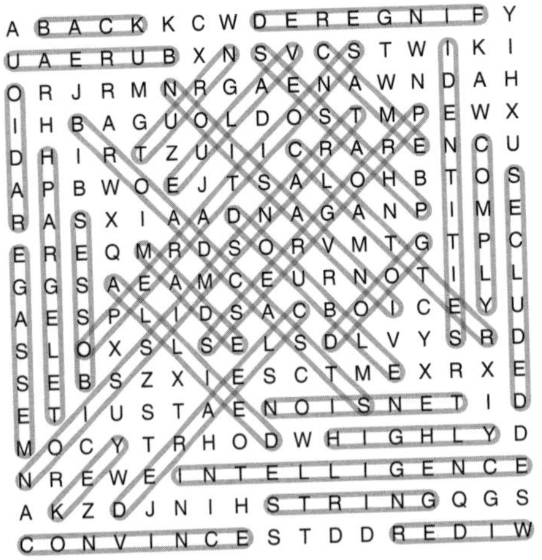

Kidnapping Frank Sinatra's Son (page 104)

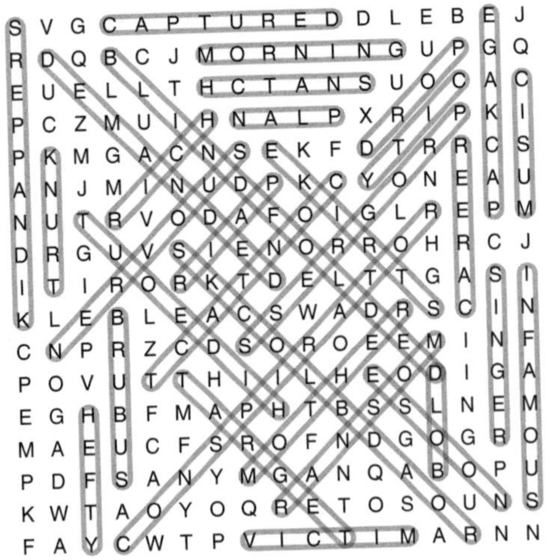

The FBI and the U.S. Criminal Code (page 102)

Machine Gun Kelly (page 106)

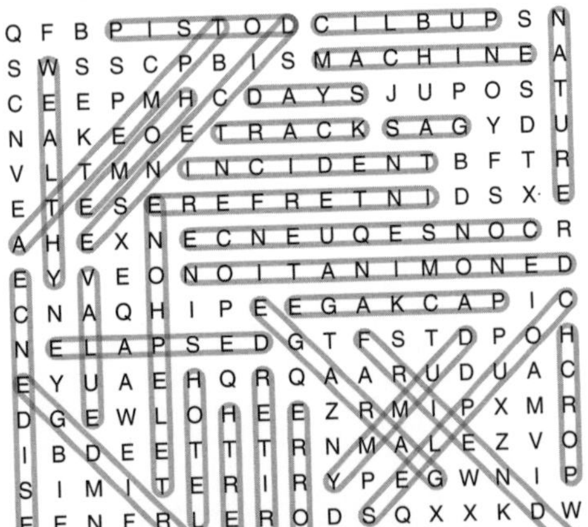

Answer Key

Gerhard Arthur Puff (page 108)

L	G	Y	U	D	E	A	D	S	U	R	R	E	N	D	E	R
P	E	N	I	T	E	N	T	I	A	R	Y	R	G	F	E	Y
T	X	E	F	E	T	A	I	C	O	S	S	A	Q	A	R	Y
X	O	I	L	O	B	B	Y	D	E	D	R	E	H	O	L	V
P	R	A	T	T	O	R	N	E	Y	N	B	P	T	R	S	X
E	Q	W	J	H	O	S	P	I	T	A	L	A	E	F	L	E
P	B	I	N	D	K	N	I	N	T	S	M	D	N	L	L	L
D	X	R	A	Q	A	D	O	T	C	R	R	Y	L	K	A	B
N	A	S	D	R	N	I	E	B	O	O	Z	A	R	D	R	A
A	H	F	R	O	T	M	W	F	S	D	B	W	E	V	E	C
H	L	O	B	I	P	G	E	I	N	W	A	R	D	H	V	O
T	W	O	S	T	Y	R	D	C	X	N	N	I	R	L	O	V
C	N	O	I	T	A	R	I	P	X	E	D	A	U	U	C	E
B	P	H	L	I	V	E	M	I	R	C	I	T	M	L	J	R
G	R	I	R	E	L	L	I	K	L	E	T	S	I	P	G	R
U	U	F	O	O	O	I	D	A	R	T	Q	F	I	D	B	I
G	P	A	I	R	T	E	S	U	O	H	E	R	A	W	Q	G

The Unabomber (page 112)

R	S	U	S	T	N	E	N	O	P	M	O	C	E	D	Q	V
E	U	N	U	P	L	U	D	J	F	I	M	F	E	E	M	F
I	I	S	A	I	E	E	E	O	I	A	V	T	S	T	O	T
G	N	N	V	A	T	R	R	I	N	J	A	S	E	D	T	W
N	E	E	V	S	S	E	F	I	N	C	A	S	L	E	I	I
S	G	T	I	E	N	P	F	E	I	Y	A	R	B	N	V	S
H	N	W	O	S	S	E	I	T	C	S	M	E	A	A	E	D
S	T	E	I	J	S	T	S	R	X	T	N	V	E	E	S	O
G	E	C	T	T	D	I	I	E	E	Z	T	I	C	L	K	M
N	C	I	O	T	H	D	A	G	S	S	Q	L	A	G	V	W
I	S	F	R	P	I	A	R	N	A	L	Z	E	R	S	G	O
L	O	C	O	O	C	R	C	E	A	T	A	D	T	D	E	R
I	J	S	R	X	E	O	W	A	B	L	O	F	N	L	N	L
A	S	O	N	A	C	H	M	D	T	M	Y	R	U	I	D	D
M	K	F	Q	P	P	S	T	B	N	C	O	S	S	U	E	O
T	P	R	I	M	I	T	I	V	E	A	H	B	I	B	R	A
J	L	J	R	E	C	L	U	S	E	D	H	S	I	S	A	B

TWA Flight 847 (page 110)

Q	G	I	C	M	A	N	E	Z	I	T	I	C	O	L	M	C
S	N	K	N	H	E	K	T	C	B	S	S	E	D	S	T	S
T	Q	R	E	F	N	G	A	L	L	K	T	W	N	E	T	B
O	C	A	R	A	O	M	A	O	U	U	E	O	B	A	H	P
P	O	D	L	E	R	R	T	T	C	A	I	E	E	U	R	O
E	L	B	A	A	F	S	M	E	S	T	S	D	H	A	O	S
E	L	D	T	I	I	E	S	A	C	O	E	S	V	C	W	E
C	A	O	E	P	R	O	R	I	T	T	H	T	A	C	N	N
I	B	F	M	G	R	P	V	E	C	I	E	R	U	Y	H	T
L	O	B	L	P	G	N	O	I	N	R	O	S	D	S	I	E
P	R	H	V	I	O	A	D	R	R	C	T	N	I	E	J	N
M	A	R	E	C	G	N	R	O	T	O	E	P	V	D	A	C
O	T	E	K	A	I	H	R	D	D	I	J	S	E	A	C	E
C	O	D	P	B	D	I	T	Y	V	L	O	G	R	N	K	D
C	R	R	P	A	S	S	E	N	G	E	R	S	A	E	I	F
A	S	U	M	T	B	L	G	N	I	T	A	E	B	R	N	L
K	F	M	S	B	U	G	G	N	I	V	I	L	T	G	G	T

Terrorist Attack in Yemen (page 114)

S	S	R	E	B	M	E	M	R	E	Y	O	R	T	S	E	D
A	G	E	I	R	W	D	E	L	X	D	E	N	N	A	L	P
I	N	S	S	E	I	E	O	C	E	K	G	W	Z	W	L	W
L	I	T	T	F	T	H	X	M	N	N	L	E	H	A	K	K
O	R	N	S	U	O	E	I	P	I	E	N	L	N	C	A	X
R	U	E	I	E	O	R	C	B	L	E	D	O	A	L	J	V
S	J	G	R	L	C	W	M	H	T	O	I	I	O	M	I	G
A	N	A	O	I	Q	O	E	W	N	T	D	N	V	C	S	U
S	I	R	R	N	B	U	O	D	I	I	G	E	T	E	W	I
L	E	D	R	G	G	R	I	D	I	S	C	I	D	A	T	D
O	N	E	E	P	K	V	D	C	I	C	M	I	T	X	A	A
C	I	L	T	G	F	A	P	D	K	S	I	E	A	R	O	N
O	M	E	X	U	I	W	E	H	N	L	R	U	Q	N	B	C
T	A	V	K	G	N	I	L	L	I	K	Y	N	S	V	S	E
O	X	A	Q	P	I	E	X	T	E	N	S	I	V	E	K	I
R	E	R	R	E	T	V	I	V	A	S	S	I	S	T	E	D
P	P	T	T	R	O	P	I	M	P	A	C	T	R	C	U	S

Answer Key

A Russian Named Zubilin

(page 116)

S	A	B	O	T	A	G	E	B	R	E	S	O	L	C	M	P
L	F	K	M	Z	L	A	I	T	N	E	T	O	P	H	U	I
A	T	R	L	S	I	G	N	I	F	I	C	A	N	T	N	Q
T	S	P	Z	U	U	L	O	E	C	N	I	V	N	O	C	U
I	A	W	M	R	E	A	S	O	N	Q	R	E	T	F	A	E
V	O	S	R	E	T	R	A	U	Q	D	A	E	H	C	U	D
T	C	P	Q	J	T	P	S	D	O	E	M	N	K	N	Q	L
Y	B	R	P	A	D	T	R	E	U	M	Q	A	B	R	A	B
P	T	E	P	O	M	A	A	G	I	P	Y	E	J	I	T	R
E	D	P	R	A	W	E	I	L	R	R	L	N	R	O	R	E
W	E	A	G	O	R	R	R	E	E	I	O	T	O	T	R	C
R	S	R	C	U	T	T	D	I	E	X	S	T	O	N	Q	E
I	U	E	Y	N	Y	I	N	V	C	U	T	W	C	R	A	I
T	C	D	I	E	C	U	A	E	D	A	N	E	W	A	O	V
T	C	X	N	A	A	B	L	N	R	S	M	N	N	I	F	E
E	A	O	T	C	L	R	I	J	L	A	I	R	E	T	A	M
N	M	E	F	E	Y	T	S	C	O	U	N	T	R	Y	L	H

German Spy Roundup

(page 120)

V	J	S	S	E	N	T	E	N	C	E	D	N	T	M	I	E
Z	E	U	N	I	A	T	P	A	C	M	O	N	G	A	N	S
C	N	O	J	R	D	H	P	O	Z	N	E	M	N	N	T	P
O	O	I	Z	T	H	T	E	V	E	G	N	B	I	U	E	Y
C	I	R	K	Z	U	C	S	H	A	Y	B	W	R	F	R	Z
E	N	T	T	R	N	O	T	E	B	O	O	K	G	A	C	S
N	A	S	E	L	D	E	B	I	R	C	S	E	D	C	E	T
S	P	U	D	S	A	N	D	E	K	C	A	R	T	T	P	N
O	M	D	J	T	U	T	O	E	Z	O	Y	Y	Y	U	T	E
R	O	N	R	A	A	O	I	I	T	E	C	O	P	R	E	M
S	C	I	I	L	I	C	I	V	T	H	L	A	U	I	D	N
O	B	C	A	S	E	L	C	R	F	O	G	T	R	N	O	G
T	G	O	L	E	A	D	S	I	E	O	M	I	T	G	G	I
H	S	P	O	O	R	T	M	H	D	T	L	Z	L	A	J	S
E	R	E	K	L	A	W	Y	A	J	E	S	L	G	E	B	S
R	I	F	I	N	A	L	L	Y	M	X	N	Y	O	G	D	A
D	I	N	F	O	R	M	A	T	I	O	N	T	M	W	S	Z

The End of Baby Face

(page 118)

B	D	E	V	I	L	S	S	E	N	T	I	W	E	H	H	I
C	E	W	S	G	N	I	L	G	G	U	M	S	S	S	J	I
H	B	A	U	Q	V	U	I	P	B	Y	F	E	W	E	V	S
G	N	M	N	N	K	E	U	N	R	A	T	L	C	X	I	G
W	A	M	O	O	D	O	L	E	S	A	T	O	E	O	V	T
O	U	U	R	M	R	E	B	I	I	P	N	T	N	D	R	T
U	T	N	T	G	R	B	R	C	N	N	E	I	L	A	D	N
N	O	I	H	V	O	O	O	W	E	E	L	C	N	E	E	E
D	M	T	E	R	E	S	U	C	O	L	V	S	T	Q	C	M
E	A	I	R	N	S	H	T	Q	I	R	P	U	N	O	A	N
D	T	O	N	A	T	I	I	S	I	O	L	U	J	O	R	R
D	I	N	W	R	O	X	A	C	R	L	G	D	H	J	T	E
U	C	O	U	N	B	O	O	T	L	E	G	G	I	N	G	V
A	T	C	S	Q	K	F	O	R	C	E	S	K	U	N	D	O
W	K	S	N	E	E	T	G	A	N	G	S	T	E	R	S	G
D	E	N	R	U	T	E	R	C	S	L	L	I	T	S	M	T
T	D	D	E	R	U	J	N	I	S	M	U	L	D	O	O	H

The Two Colonels

(page 122)

E	H	O	R	E	M	O	C	W	E	N	B	Q	S	A	F	D
M	E	F	E	S	U	R	L	Q	U	A	R	T	E	R	S	I
S	S	F	H	T	S	C	O	L	O	N	E	L	V	J	X	P
O	A	I	C	A	F	U	A	L	T	E	R	N	A	T	E	R
V	C	C	A	T	L	G	O	H	S	A	C	R	V	W	N	O
I	F	E	T	E	A	E	O	V	D	C	E	D	P	R	A	P
E	E	R	S	M	G	S	E	E	Z	P	P	A	F	E	I	O
T	I	M	U	E	H	N	L	F	L	E	R	Z	O	V	L	S
R	R	D	M	N	J	E	U	I	F	T	D	D	R	I	I	A
N	B	X	A	T	G	Q	E	O	Y	O	P	N	C	R	V	L
V	R	L	Z	A	M	D	A	F	L	K	C	N	E	D	I	X
E	Q	U	T	E	G	N	A	R	R	A	E	R	P	R	C	T
V	S	I	D	O	S	W	O	R	B	E	Y	E	W	L	E	R
W	O	L	S	D	T	W	E	E	D	S	X	E	A	E	R	P
N	F	I	A	T	Y	T	N	O	R	F	K	M	R	R	S	N
N	D	E	I	F	R	K	R	A	M	E	R	T	E	A	M	Q
E	C	A	L	P	R	H	O	U	S	E	S	D	K	F	V	Y

Answer Key

Guenther Rumrich (page 124)

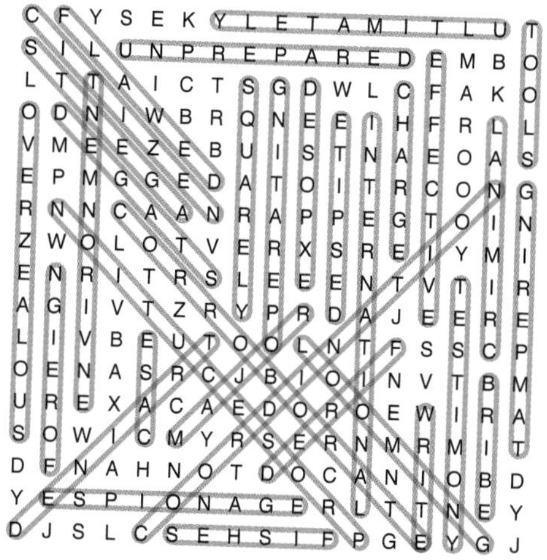

The Touhy Gang (page 128)

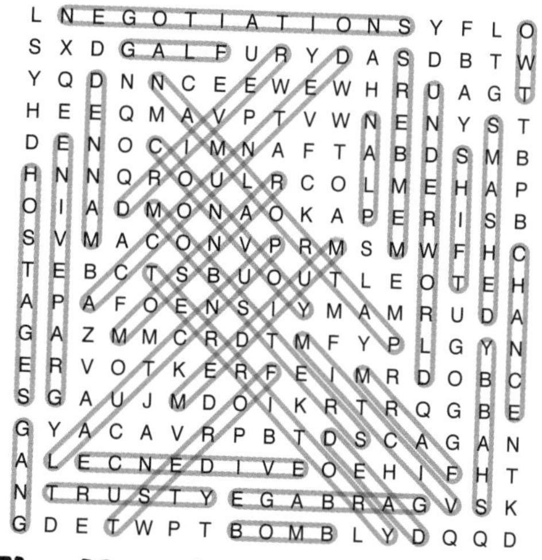

Corruption Waltzes Out (page 126)

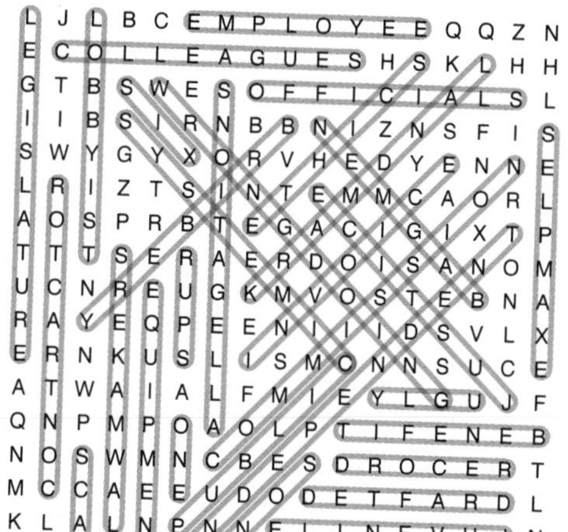

The Morris Worm (page 130)

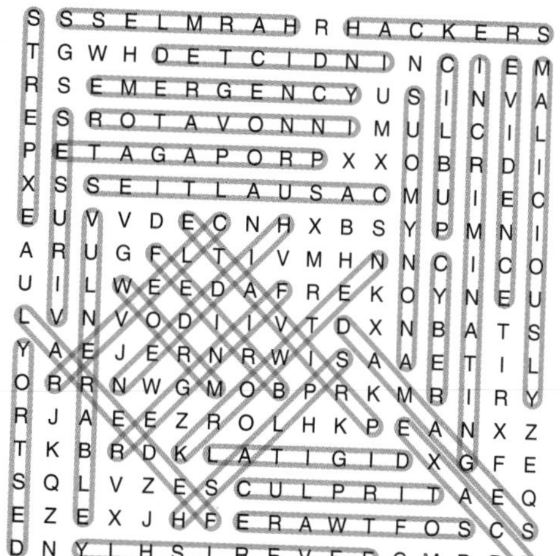

Answer Key

Alfred Brady and the Gang (page 132)

I	F	G	S	N	O	I	T	A	D	E	R	P	E	D	J	N
Y	U	A	M	M	U	N	I	T	I	O	N	E	V	O	R	D
R	D	N	T	G	N	I	B	B	O	R	D	T	X	Y	I	A
L	E	G	Q	E	R	E	T	T	A	L	T	R	L	T	P	C
E	S	H	O	L	D	U	P	S	X	N	I	A	N	S	X	O
W	P	H	W	E	L	D	E	R	S	N	N	O	S	R	R	A
E	E	T	I	D	N	A	B	T	S	I	I	S	N	I	E	L
J	R	H	N	I	J	Y	E	T	M	T	E	M	O	H	N	I
D	A	H	H	I	Z	P	I	I	C	I	E	Y	I	T	N	T
T	D	Y	H	A	F	T	R	I	T	M	M	C	T	D	A	I
N	O	A	R	A	U	C	D	I	B	O	M	N	A	O	M	O
C	E	C	T	T	E	S	V	E	O	M	E	A	L	O	A	N
H	S	H	I	S	I	I	R	R	U	L	P	R	O	L	G	W
A	E	O	C	R	T	S	R	R	O	A	D	G	I	B	R	L
R	N	A	U	C	N	A	D	T	R	F	E	A	V	B	H	Y
G	P	J	A	H	B	E	S	T	Z	R	Y	V	Q	X	T	I
E	M	O	O	T	R	P	R	O	S	E	C	U	T	I	V	E

Sabotage in Zambia (page 136)

S	C	P	R	O	B	A	T	I	O	N	C	D	Z	L	Z	U
N	O	E	S	S	O	L	D	T	M	O	E	B	Y	F	P	T
W	O	R	O	V	B	T	T	A	N	Z	O	Z	Y	S	U	P
L	P	U	O	K	I	R	R	D	I	E	V	O	W	E	R	U
O	E	S	K	M	A	K	I	L	A	N	M	I	U	Z	C	R
Y	R	A	Q	V	E	T	A	E	B	Y	N	Y	F	C	H	R
O	A	E	E	T	I	R	E	G	O	G	G	F	A	S	A	E
R	T	L	S	O	U	C	D	D	R	C	P	A	E	P	S	T
T	E	P	N	T	N	Y	S	I	T	I	O	I	L	I	E	N
S	G	S	A	E	N	M	M	R	P	E	T	P	R	I	H	I
E	I	N	T	A	O	S	T	B	R	I	P	A	P	L	B	C
D	B	N	M	T	E	E	S	A	R	Y	I	L	R	E	V	I
W	E	I	S	R	S	A	W	O	Q	L	B	B	Z	O	R	G
S	T	U	V	T	S	D	H	G	R	H	I	B	T	K	I	U
E	C	I	I	I	R	T	V	O	C	W	O	U	O	I	R	I
C	C	F	V	A	U	S	A	K	R	O	W	N	R	L	M	S
E	Y	E	H	A	A	D	S	S	K	C	O	L	C	U	J	E

Making a Racket (page 134)

J	O	C	H	R	A	C	K	E	T	E	E	R	S	C	N	S
C	O	O	J	U	S	T	I	C	E	S	E	S	O	A	W	N
H	O	N	A	R	X	E	Q	E	T	T	E	M	T	Y	E	O
W	S	S	P	E	L	A	M	E	U	C	M	I	S	T	X	I
S	T	P	A	S	D	P	N	B	R	U	L	E	R	I	T	S
E	A	I	T	T	I	C	I	E	N	O	E	V	E	L	O	I
T	B	R	H	R	H	R	T	I	P	X	M	I	L	A	R	V
A	K	A	E	A	T	L	C	O	P	A	R	T	A	T	T	O
D	C	C	T	I	Y	A	R	E	N	I	L	I	E	U	I	R
N	I	Y	I	N	T	T	R	H	A	I	C	G	D	R	O	P
A	R	D	C	I	E	I	U	L	A	L	I	U	D	B	N	S
M	B	U	O	M	E	N	F	J	J	P	D	F	G	T	N	N
S	L	N	I	N	T	I	M	I	D	A	T	I	O	N	E	O
A	A	Y	C	E	E	T	A	N	I	M	L	U	C	K	M	I
E	N	E	X	O	N	H	A	P	H	A	Z	A	R	D	U	N
L	E	E	E	V	I	T	C	E	T	O	R	P	Z	F	C	U
P	P	Q	H	O	S	E	I	R	A	G	A	V	B	R	A	G

The Osage Indian Murders (page 138)

B	I	A	Y	E	T	A	V	I	R	P	V	D	I	D	G	C
A	N	K	A	C	S	L	A	C	O	L	E	N	M	U	U	R
W	H	E	R	E	W	R	I	H	L	B	R	A	T	A	B	E
N	E	M	H	C	N	E	H	A	M	O	T	D	Z	R	N	A
R	R	Y	E	L	R	G	U	O	T	T	E	D	S	F	O	T
D	I	P	K	P	U	S	B	C	E	I	E	D	R	L	I	I
E	T	O	T	W	O	M	E	R	L	B	I	D	E	A	T	V
C	T	W	U	U	F	P	O	I	I	S	E	D	T	W	C	E
O	E	E	G	N	S	J	F	R	T	K	V	T	S	Y	E	Q
M	L	R	A	O	D	K	B	R	O	L	Y	I	I	E	N	U
P	L	D	R	L	I	E	U	O	F	U	A	V	S	R	N	K
O	U	P	O	L	M	S	R	E	H	A	P	Y	Q	Y	O	H
S	B	A	L	C	T	C	Q	T	N	T	M	E	O	U	C	I
E	F	E	N	F	T	H	S	N	A	I	L	I	S	R	H	R
D	R	G	U	V	H	O	W	L	W	K	V	A	L	L	C	E
B	D	L	B	G	A	V	R	P	E	P	E	A	E	Y	A	D
F	U	H	E	R	B	A	L	W	A	W	R	R	R	W	X	F

Answer Key

Nazi Saboteurs in America (page 140)

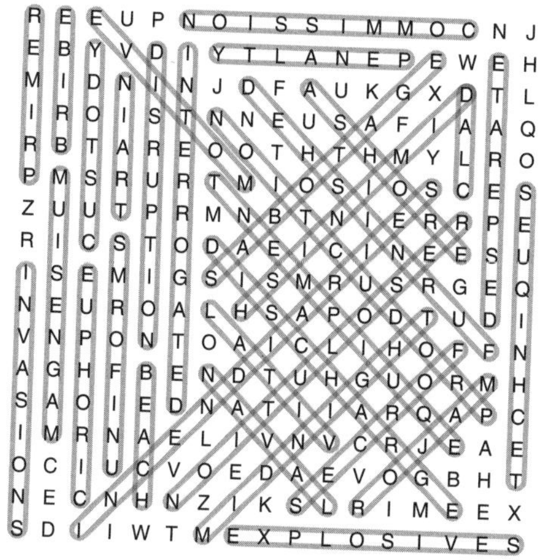

Operation Innocent Images (page 144)

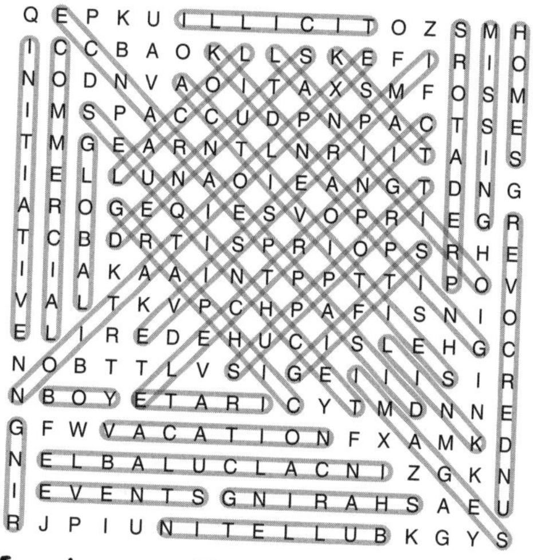

The Elizabeth Short Murder (page 142)

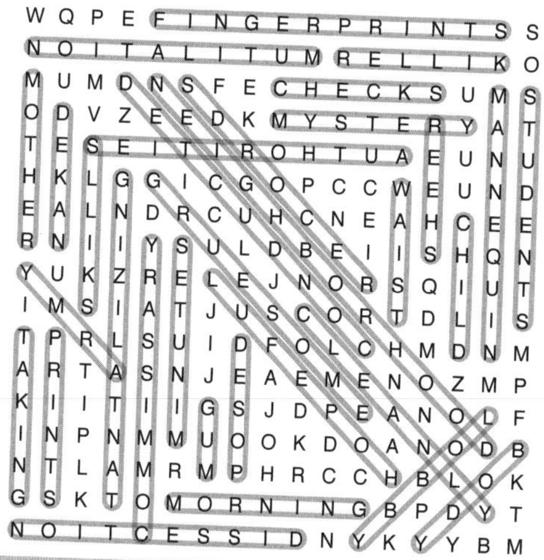

Mortgage Fraud Takedown (page 146)

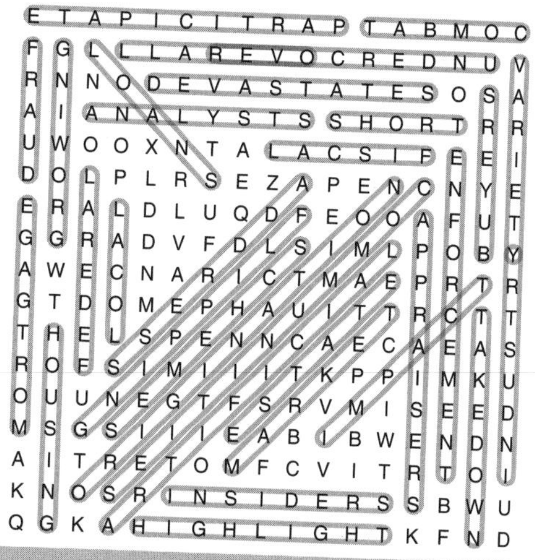

Answer Key

Radical Bombs and the Red Scare (page 148)

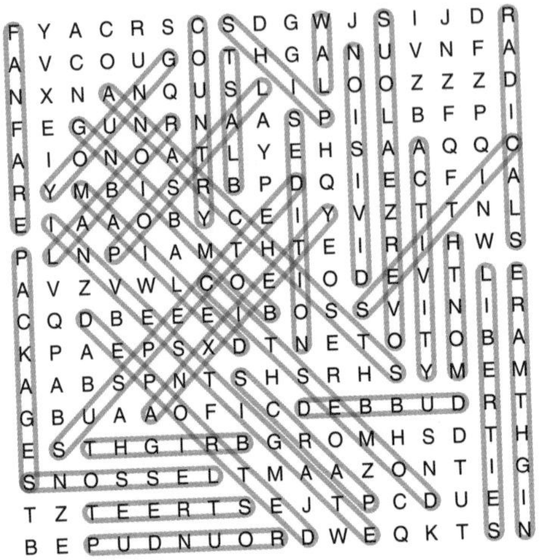

A Front Page Kidnapping (page 152)

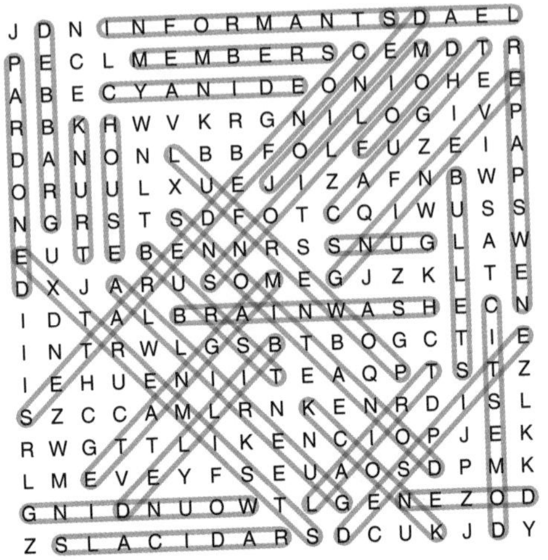

Pan Am Flight 103 (page 150)

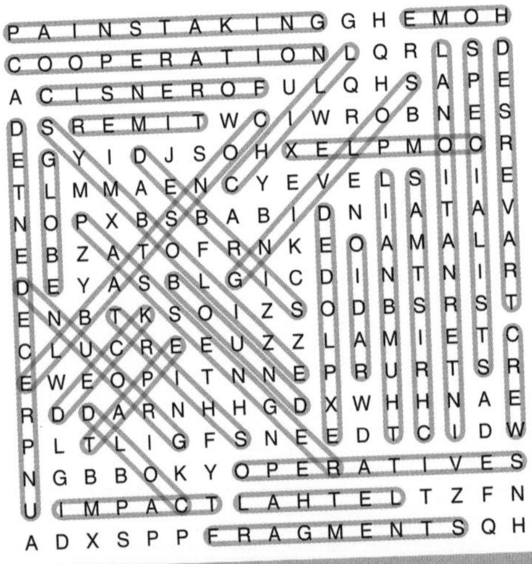

The Spy of Pearl Harbor (page 154)

Answer Key

The Pizza Connection
(page 156)

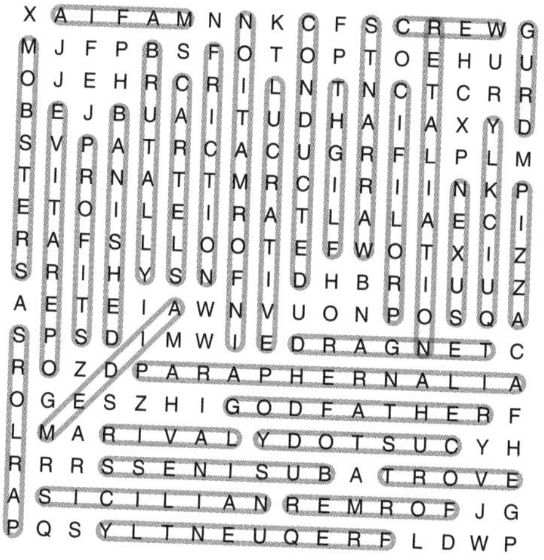

Timothy McVeigh
(page 160)

Nussbaum and Wilcoxson
(page 158)

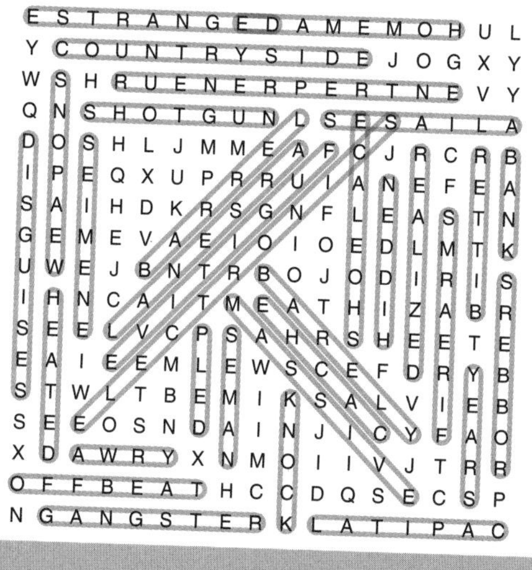

Operation Greylord
(page 162)

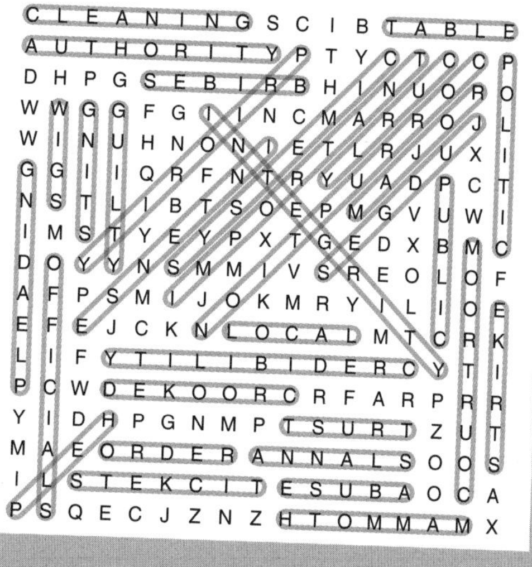

Answer Key

Fraud in the Defense Department (page 164)

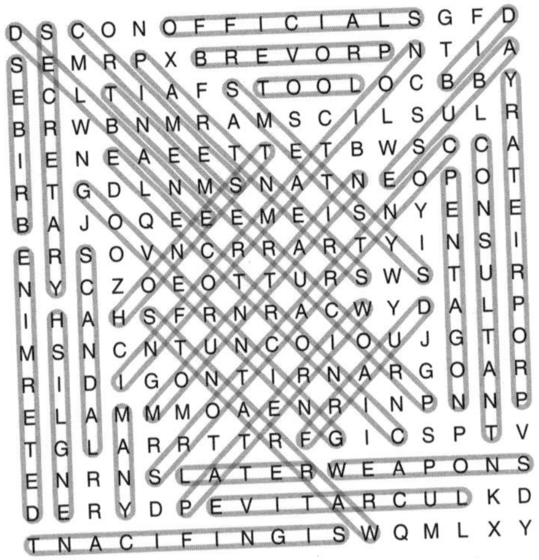

The UAF 855 Hijacking (page 168)

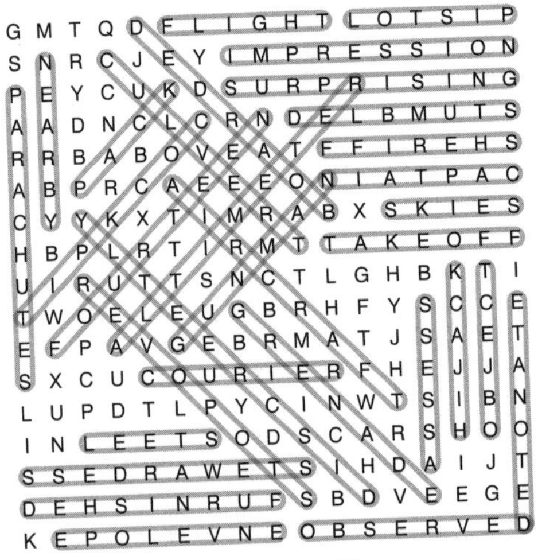

Pine Ridge Murders (page 166)

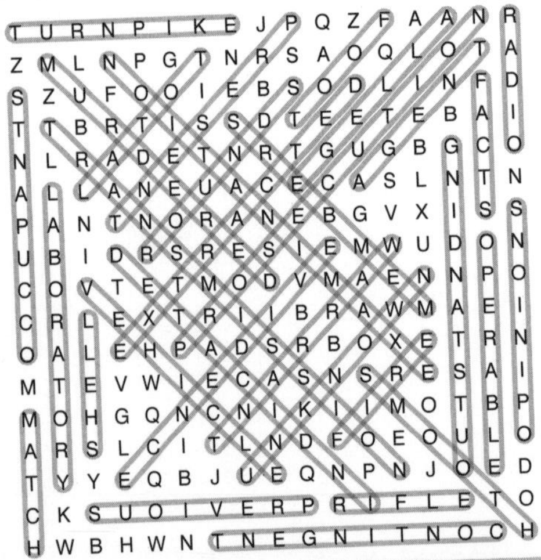

An FBI Betrayal (page 170)

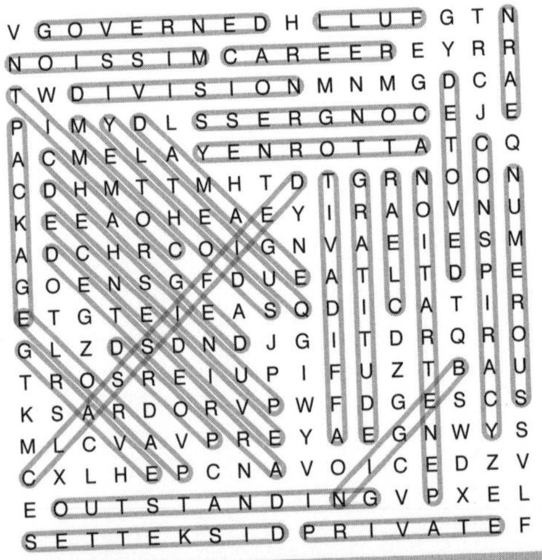